DERAILED

The Betrayal of the National Dream

D1497338

971
.0647
Ber

1188

Bercuson, David Jay, 1945-
    Derailed : the betrayal of the national dream /
David J. Bercuson and Barry Cooper. -- Toronto : Key
Porter Books, c1994.
    213 p.

07466528   ISBN:1550135732 (pbk.)

1. Canada - Politics and government - 1984-1993. I.
Cooper, Barry, 1943- II. Title

1795   94SEP24   06/ex   1-00635834

DERAILED
The Betrayal of the National Dream

David J. Bercuson

and

Barry Cooper

KEY PORTER·BOOKS

Canadian Cataloguing in Publication Data

Bercuson, David Jay, 1945-
        Derailed: the betrayal of the national dream

Includes index.
ISBN 1-55013-573-2

1. Canada — Politics and government — 1984-1993.
I. Cooper, Barry, 1943- . II. Title.

FC630.B47 1994   971.064'7   C94-931449-8
F1034.2.B47 1994

The publisher gratefully acknowledges the assistance of the Canada Council and the Government of Ontario.

Key Porter Books Limited
70 The Esplanade
Toronto, Ontario
Canada M5E 1R2

Printed and bound in Canada

94 95 96 97 98 5 4 3 2 1

This book is dedicated to John A. Macdonald,
George-Etienne Cartier, and the Fathers of Confederation.
They *did* build better than they knew;
it's just that so many of their successors did not.

ACKNOWLEDGEMENTS

The authors are grateful to Peter Archambault, who helped to do the
research for this book, and to Michael Bliss who was kind enough to read
portions of the manuscript.

Table of Contents

Introduction

O h Canada! We stand on guard for thee? Not
likely; not lately.

Consider a typical week in the life of this
country. On Tuesday, February 22, 1994, the
federal finance minister announced that his
new budget will have a deficit of *only* $39.7 billion — which will
add just that much to a national debt already over $500 billion.
The minister thought he had accomplished something great. On
Thursday, February 24, the provincial treasurer of Alberta
announced that his budget would cut the provincial deficit by half
and that he was on target to a no-deficit budget by 1997. That was
two days after the Calgary Board of Education had announced
mass firings of teachers and more to come. Pensioners, educators,
municipal politicians, and others began to rally against the Alberta
budget, even though in the June 1993 provincial election the vast
majority of Albertans had voted either for "massive cuts," the Tory

election pledge, or for "brutal cuts," which the Liberals had promised. Debt now dominates the Canadian political agenda, but there is still no consensus about how to tackle it and everyone seems to want to tackle it at someone else's expense.

In that same week the national jobless rate in Canada continued to stand at over 11 per cent, and the federal government held out little hope for improvement over the next three years. Canada's jobless rate has been that high for so long, and with so little prospect of coming under 10 per cent anytime soon, that it no longer makes headlines when someone such as the hapless Kim Campbell, prime minister for a day, points out the obvious: Canada has the highest continuing rate of unemployment among the member nations of the Organization for Economic Cooperation and Development (basically the western industrialized countries). Entire sections of Canada are sustained by Unemployment Insurance; whole communities in Atlantic Canada have lived for decades on what they cynically label the federal 10/42 Plan; work for ten straight weeks and live on Unemployment Insurance for the next forty-two. Now, with the new federal budget, that will become the 12/40 Plan. Much better.

That was the same week that Ontario announced it would cut its tobacco taxes by just over $9 per carton to match the cuts already made by Quebec and to add to the $5-per-carton tax cut implemented by Ottawa some weeks before. That action followed the spectacle of the open sale of smuggled cigarettes on the streets of Quebec by tobacco merchants fed up with losing business to the illegal sale of smuggled cigarettes on Mohawk reserves in Quebec and Ontario. The lucrative smuggled cigarette market was created holus-bolus by high taxes on tobacco. But then, there are high taxes on liquor also. And the Canadian tax revolt, which of course the government denies is happening, goes far beyond cigarettes.

There is wholesale tax dodging throughout Canada, and some estimates put the size of the underground economy at $90 billion dollars. The truth is as simple as it is stark; if Canadians were paying the taxes they are legally obliged to pay, including tobacco tax, liquor tax, the GST, and income taxes, the deficit would disappear almost overnight.

Why did the wholesale smuggling of cigarettes go on as long as it did? For two reasons. First, and most obviously, because Canadian tobacco companies exported hundreds of millions of dollars of duty-free cigarettes to the United States (even though Americans detest Canadian cigarettes) where they could be bought tax free and smuggled back to Canada. When accused of complicity in the illegal cigarette trade, the tobacco companies pleaded ignorance. They were as ignorant of the result of their exports to the United States as the piano player is who pleads he doesn't know what's going on in the upstairs bedrooms of the whorehouse. He just plays the tunes; they just shipped the smokes.

The second reason cigarette smuggling became endemic is because the federal government refused to lift a hand to stop it. Most of the cigarettes smuggled into Canada were brought into the country through Mohawk reserves that straddle the Canada-U.S. border. Members of the Mohawk Warrior societies dared the federal government to come on to their "self-governing" reserves to stop the smuggling. They threatened armed resistance. They claimed that the "cigarette trade," as it was euphemistically called, was creating jobs on the reserves and self-respect among their people. At one point, they even fired with impunity at a Canadian Armed Forces helicopter that dared stray into their "sovereign" airspace! By strutting about with illegal weapons, a few hundred Mohawk Warriors cowed the national government of twenty-seven million Canadians into a de facto admission that Mohawk reserves are little sovereign satraps exempt from Canadian law. Maybe the next job-creating, self-respect-engendering activity we'll see on those reserves will be cocaine processing. Certain it is that the Mohawk Warriors know the right people.

That same week the Canadian recession continued and the weakness of the Canadian economy was reflected in a falling Canadian dollar. Although the U.S. economy had been roaring out of recession for at least eight months, and chalking up phenomenal growth figures in the last quarter of 1993, Canada's "recovery" had been positively anaemic. It used to be the case that a strong U.S. economy would invariably mean good economic growth in Canada as well, but no more. That is because, for the most part, the United States is way ahead of Canada in research and development, in taking advantage of technological advances, in balancing environmental needs with the need for economic growth, in creating and sustaining strategic low-tax but high-quality investing environments, in taking advantage of overseas market opportunities, and in extolling the work ethic among its people. So, Canadians, living in a nation bloated by expensive and useless welfare schemes, face another year of increasing taxes (or user fees, or medicare premiums, or tuition fees, which all amount to the same thing), no increases in real income, and a poorer level of services, while Americans look forward to an increase in their living standards.

Anyone tuning in to the parliamentary channel that week would have seen some strange spectacles. The leader of Her Majesty's Loyal Opposition is a man whose avowed aim is to lead Quebec out of Canada. One of his main contributions to political debate was his charge that the Canadian Olympic hockey team did not have enough Quebeckers; he was silent when Quebec athletes won most of Canada's Olympic medals! At the same time, The

Reform party was accused of racism when it attacked a former Liberal MP for continuing to sit in the house even after revelations that he had (1) told his former employers that he wished they had been additional victims of a killer who had murdered 14 women students at the University of Montreal and (2) claimed to be a lawyer when he is not. The official opposition, the Bloc Quebecois , was also attacked for racism when it dared to suggest that Ottawa ought to enforce Canadian laws on Aboriginal reserves. Of course, being separatist, members of the Bloc don't particularly like Canadian laws and want to live in a country governed by Quebec law.

What in the world has happened to Canada? At the end of World War Two, 1.1 million Canadian men and women returned from overseas having played a proud part in the defeat of Nazi Germany. With a total population of just over 12 million people, Canada had created an army, navy, and air force virtually from scratch and had shouldered a heavy burden in the Allied victory in the west. At home, Canada had become an "arsenal of democracy" in its own right, and the products of Canadian forests, factories, and fields had helped sustain the Allies through six years of bitter warfare. Canada's new stature was acknowledged by the nations of the world when it was elected to membership on the United Nations Security Council in late 1947 and when it was asked by Britain and the United States in early 1948 to join a secret three-nation discussion that eventually led to the creation of NATO in 1949. In fact, Canada was one of only three nations on earth in 1945 with the capability of building an atomic bomb and was a charter member (and, for a time, chair) of the International Atomic Energy Agency.

Canadians faced huge problems in 1945: the nation was clearly under-populated, but many Canadians were biased against immigration; war spending had piled up a massive debt and there were few consumer goods available; the future was uncertain; a massive dollar imbalance with the United States created a serious fiscal crisis in 1947-48; union demands for higher postwar wages led to a rash of strikes in major industries; world peace seemed threatened by a growing Cold War with the USSR. But Canadians did not seem especially worried. They rolled up their sleeves with an infectious energy and enthusiasm, convinced that they lived in the best country in the world. They got married, had kids, bought houses and cars and washing machines, went to school, and took part in a prolonged period of economic growth with rising living standards and virtually no inflation. They also enjoyed a rudimentary welfare state that provided protection against economic disaster. But they did not rely on government to make everything right; they paid their taxes, kept the peace, and built a strong and united country. For a time it must have seemed as if Wilfrid Laurier had been right when he had proclaimed that the twentieth century would belong to Canada.

Those times are now a memory that grows dimmer with each passing year. Today Canada is a country that has lost virtually all sense of community and direction. We daily waste the talents and energies of millions of Canadians. We are losing our sense of good citizenship. We seem afraid to say what we believe, to affirm and fight for what we know to be right, and to condemn and fight against what we know to be wrong. We have forgotten that people must do things for themselves and not rely on others or on government for their well-being. We have lost our sense of destiny. We are throwing away the chance to live in what could be the most democratic, most balanced, most fair, most reasonable place on earth. We have become a nation of whiners, demanding to be taken care of from cradle to grave and afraid to strike out on our own. We have become enamoured of failure, afraid of success, and worshipful of under-achievement. We have become a nation of losers.

There are remedies to our economic and political problems; they are thrown at us daily in books, magazines, and in the media. Cut budgets. Abolish welfare. Spend less. Reform UI. Ban any constitutional discussion for the next two thousand years. Elect honest men and women to office and throw out the rascals. But nothing will work unless Canadians recover or rediscover the basic purposes and the spirit of achievement that built this country in the first place. We have lost our pride in trying solely to serve our interests. To begin to recover it we must start by taking a long hard look at the road that led us to where we are now. Before we can fix it, we must know what went wrong with our country.

1
Thinking About the Mess

In the prologue to the first volume of his memoirs, Sir Harold Macmillan told the following story. After the defeat of the Conservatives in 1945, Winston Churchill, now leader of the opposition, entertained his front-bench colleagues at fortnightly lunches at the Savoy Hotel. "At one of these," wrote Macmillan, "there was brought a rather equivocal and shapeless pudding, which he viewed with some distaste. He called the waiter. 'Pray take away this pudding. It has no theme.'" Macmillan added that he always remembered the event as "a warning to authors as well as to cooks." It is a warning we have tried to heed in this book.

Our theme, broadly stated, is that the character of Canadian political and, indeed, economic and social life has changed for the worse since the end of World War Two. There may be persons abroad in the land for whom this proposition is not self-evidently true. If so, we eagerly await correction in gross or in detail. In the last half century, we say, something has gone terribly wrong in Canada. We aim here to show what and how, and perhaps even why. When we speak of the character of Canadian political life, we intend nothing mysterious, obscure, or even academic. We are attempting to bring some unity to a mass of institutional and ideological detail, to discern a theme lurking behind an array of particulars, a theme that marshals them and indicates their meaning and significance.

With human beings, we can see a unity or identity of the body in youth and age because the shape or form or organization persists even if the materials that compose it change. In individual bodies, so with bodies politic: there exists an obvious and intelligible unity over the last half century of our history, despite changes in governing parties, the structure of the economy, and the demographic profile of our citizens. The unity we have in mind is that of a coherence of meaning, or a habitual inclination, but it does not exclude diversity, ambivalence, or change. One might even speak of a "tradition," although the tradition we are speaking of is perverse, unstable, and self-destructive, which is not what traditions usually are. Indeed, the purpose of tradition is usually to shelter human beings from exactly the alien and dangerous winds of change that Canadians have conjured all on their own.

One way of indicating the character of postwar Canada is to portray two contrasting tendencies. One of them has, on the whole, served us well, in that it has contributed to the prosperity of Canadians and to their sense of political contentment, if not to their happiness. It has also allowed Canadians to form those warm communities of meaning that give them a sense of place and a feeling of identity. The other, which increasingly we have followed, has promised us happiness and especially security but has provided neither and has landed us in our current mess — a condition in which we lack both economic prosperity and political unity and have no compensating feelings of purpose or collective goodwill.

The ideological roots of these contrasting tendencies can be traced to any number of famous texts in Western political philosophy and may be summarized as the opposition between the doctrine of a natural or spontaneous harmony in society that is achieved without state or bureaucratic intervention and the doctrine that human interests can be identified only by means of political regulation. To employ a more or less conventional vocabulary, the first alternative is liberal or libertarian, the second collectivist or communitarian. (The term "pseudo-communitarian" is perhaps more accurate, but unwieldy.) We should say at the outset that we are using these labels as a kind of shorthand and as a way of highlighting patterns and making sense of things.

The liberal stresses the importance of individuality, that is, the rights of the individual and his or her freedom from both social supervision and political control. Edmund Burke, who is often called a conservative, spoke as a liberal when he praised the freedom of Englishmen as their patrimony. That a conservative may be a liberal is no paradox when the thing to be conserved is liberty. The usual array of liberties deemed worthy of conservation include: the right to be tried by due process of law; to be taxed only after a parliament where there was freedom to debate had consented; to meet publicly in association to discuss and to submit a petition to the government in defence of one's interests; and, perhaps most fundamental of all, to acquire, use, and dispose of one's property.

The emphasis on individuality implies for liberals that the power, right, and authority of government is limited. State action is for liberals, in the words of Walter Bagehot in his work *The Eng-*

lish Constitution, "alien action ... an imposed tyranny from without, not ... the consummated result of our own organized wishes." Moreover, any concentration of power is likely to be dangerous to individual choice and activity. Governments should therefore be watched closely. For liberals, John Philpot Curran was right two centuries ago when he observed: "The condition upon which God hath given liberty to man is eternal vigilance; which condition if he break, servitude is at once the consequence of his crime, and the punishment of his guilt." Both federalism and the separation of powers are welcomed by liberals as institutional means of dispersing power and authority and thereby providing greater opportunities for the expression of individuality or of personality.

Finally, liberalism embodies its anti-statist sentiments in the doctrine of the rule of law. This means three things. First, wide discretionary powers are removed from the hands of government. Powers of constraint can therefore be exercised only for breach of the law that has been established in the usual way before a court. Second, all citizens are equal before the law. There are by law neither second-class citizens nor privileged aristocrats. As the great English legal theorist A.V. Dicey insisted, this was especially true for public functionaries. Third, governments, including the courts, exist in order to secure rights, not to create them (for rights exist by nature) and not to exercise them on behalf of citizens.

In contrast, collectivism disputes each of the positions and arguments of liberalism. Its most impressive characteristic is an intense and focal concern with the public good, the public interest, or the collective good — different names used by collectivists to mean the same thing. Liberals stress that justice depends upon individual autonomy and achievement and especially the protection of one's freedom to do as one will with one's own; collectivists are of the opinion, first, that a community exists and that its interests are morally superior (and so to be preferred) to those of the individual. Justice, for them, is first of all a collective concern. Liberals, too, have always paid some attention to collective concerns — in regard to defence and the protection of property, for instance. But there is an important contrast and difference in priority. Collectivists are especially fond of the promotion of "social justice," the chief component of which is security. Instead of emphasizing freedom of opportunity or freedom of contract, whatever the consequences for social, economic, and political equality, collectivists focus on the desirability of social, economic, and political parity. Parity is sometimes seen as a collective or group right to equal outcomes, and is justified as a matter of administrative convenience. Collectivists say that it is both easier and fairer not to have to make distinctions (or *invidious* distinctions, the collectivist would say) or to tolerate private and regional interests or initiatives. More to the point, as uniform treatment and equal outcomes are incrementally attained, any remaining dissimilarities or inequalities are considered to be ever more unacceptable and unjust. Decentralization is viewed not as a safeguard against government power but as an opportunity for local deviance and so for injustice. Freedom, likewise, is understood as not the absence of legal or social constraint but the attainment of a life the reasonableness of which can be defined beforehand. Sometimes this is called strategic planning.

The great instrument for attaining collectivist goals is, of course, the state. If this entails increased supervision, it is a price the collectivist willingly pays. Or rather, he or she does not regard such supervision as a price: it is the actualization of public virtue. Public authorities are called upon to supervise economic activities, to do more for the individual through social welfare services, and thereby to promote — indeed to create and sustain — public harmony.

Otherwise, the collectivist says, public harmony would not exist. Individual claims are, in principle, and so by intention, permanently subordinated to social needs.

It is the intervention of the state and of state agencies that accounts for the ersatz nature of this so-called communitarian doctrine. Real communitarians are advocates of real communities. And real communities — that is, narrow, local, prejudiced, hierarchic, closed, face-to-face groups of human beings, villages whose inhabitants know one another intensely and distrust all outsiders — have practically disappeared not only from Canada but from the modern world. Supposed communitarians and genuine collectivists may well be animated by dreams of romantic village life where all members cooperate and help. Indeed, on occasion, clever intellectuals have evoked the image of a "helping society" as the one thing needful. Many less clever individuals have gone along with such dreams. And dreams we take them to be, because in Canada today we belong to a modern society not a premodern community. This is not to deny that we may have lost much in the change from the one to the other. It is simply to acknowledge what is.

In exposing these contrasting positions we do not seek simply to act as advocates of one or the other, though it should by now be clear that we do not dream of, or hope for, cooperative communities as a basis for developing a workable public policy. We do not accept the postmodern vogue for seeing all events as opportunities for personal growth; nor do we believe that there are no such things as criminals or that differences matter so little that no one can say, "This is stupid!" Apart from excluding dreams, especially the half-baked and pipe variety, we have tried to be sensible and to avoid dogmatism. Where we advocate a specific course, we realize that putting it into operation will depend on circumstances and opportunities. And yet, one must aim at something. What we think a reasonable target will become clear soon enough. In any event, there is a wide range of intermediate possibilities between the liberal and the communitarian visions.

Historically speaking, as we shall see, advocates of one side have the greatest appeal when practitioners of the other side are in the saddle. In his essay, "Coleridge," written in 1840, J.S. Mill, a moderate individualist or moderate communitarian, provided a useful example. He noted that, during the eighteenth century, many Englishmen thought that the government ought to make itself as inconspicuous as possible. "The cry of the people was not `help us,' 'guide us,' 'do for us the things we cannot do, and instruct us, that we may do well those which we can....' — The cry was 'let us alone.'" And the reason was that the government was attempting to do things for which it was ill-equipped and unsuited. As a result it was despised as rapacious and viewed with contempt.

If similar cries are raised today, it is not necessarily because liberalism appeals to all reasonable men and women, but that reasonable citizens find that the "help," the "guidance," the "instruction" that governments have provided have proven futile, misguided, perverse, or no longer needed or wanted. In any case, it is a rare liberal who repudiates *all* regulation of society or the provision of *any* social services. Communitarians, on the other hand, seem to be less restrained by the bounds of common sense.

A subtheme of this book is that communitarians in Canada, seduced by the confidence that comes from long incumbency in positions of power, have been less willing to acknowledge limits to what they can do than liberals have been to acknowledge that the government can do at least a few things well. As we shall see, challenges to individualism have been issued in the name of the public good in such a way that collectivists and communitarians don the robes of velvet tyrants. And when they do, liberals resume their search for alternatives. In the story that follows, it will become clear that these two tendencies are not identified explicitly with either of the two parties that have formed governments, the Liberals and the Progressive Conservatives. As for the other parties, the NDP may be more in the collectivist camp and the Reform Party may be pretty much libertarian, but neither has yet attained the status of a party that has a reasonable chance to form the government. Nor, of course, has the Bloc Québécois (and who can say what future, if any, the Tories will have?). In any case, as we shall see soon enough, political parties are responsible for only one part of what went wrong.

There are a few obvious indicators of the growth of collectivism. Identifying one of them as early as the mid-1840s, the London *Times* editorialized that, in "session after session we are amplifying the province of the Legislature, and asserting its moral prerogatives. Parliament aspires to be the *pater patriae*, and is for laying aside the policeman, the gaoler, and the executioner, in exchange for the more kindly and dignified functions of the father, the schoolmaster, and the friend." In Canada today we give voice to the triumph of the "kindly and dignified functions" of the government with a bitter irony born of experience. "I'm from the government, and I'm here to help you," has become a sick joke. Indeed, we have now moved from an at least dignified and stern paternal government to a thoroughly undignified and suffocating maternal one.

Public Spending

The first and most important indicator of how and how much government has "helped" Canadians can be found in public expenditures. For most of us it is no accident that the chief contact we have with the government is through Revenue Canada or its guardian agency, Customs and Excise. The collectivist logic is clear and straightforward and so, too, has been the libertarian response.

Unless prices fall, extending government activity is bound to cost more. That is why a good indicator of increased collectivism is increased public expenditure. Increased public expenditure means either increased revenue and taxation or increased debt. As Canadians have recently seen, it sometimes means an increase in all three. This kind of increase has always been viewed by liberals as malignant, as prima facie evidence of losses in freedom. The argument is simple and has remained more or less unchanged for the past two centuries: those in power use that power to extend the reach of government so as to ensure that the things people ought to do for themselves are done for them by officials, who are put in place by politicians and paid by taxpayers. The reasons have varied, from the need to provide protective administrative oversight for complex economic and technological changes to the belief that the government could do a better job than was already being done. In any particular instance, the arguments of the collectivists might be plausible enough. One should bear in mind, however, that this is not simply because of their pure reasonableness but because of circumstances as well. The times may appear to be sufficiently out of joint as to make the appeal to the state to "do something" a reasonable one. The most obvious example is war and insurrection. No reasonable citizen can doubt that under such circumstances the state necessarily and temporarily takes on an increased presence in everyone's life. But when circumstances change, the continued existence of programs that were reasonable enough when initiated may be quite unreasonable. Conscription in time of war, for example, may be a reasonable policy; but that does not mean it will be equally reasonable in time of peace.

In any event, all observers seem to agree that there has been an enormous increase in the amount of money raised and spent by the federal, provincial, and municipal governments during the past half century. The rate of growth has changed over the years and charting those changes is important, but the direction has remained the same. Consider some recent figures: in 1970, total government spending amounted to about $31 billion; by 1988 it was $271 billion, a 775 per cent increase. During the same period the total income of the country increased by 577 per cent. This means that government spending has absorbed ever greater amounts of the gross domestic product or GDP — the total spending power generated in the country. In simple terms, the government slice of the GDP pie has grown from about 35 per cent in 1970 to 45 per cent in 1988. Or, to put it another way, citizens and taxpayers have surrendered control of about half their income to the government.

When one looks at changes in the kinds of things that governments spend money on, the trend towards collectivism is even more clear. In 1970 the top category for expenditure was education, closely followed by social welfare, which in our scheme of things includes all transfer payments to individuals: old age pensions, family allowances, unemployment insurance benefits, and welfare. By 1988, social welfare was in top spot, absorbing nearly a quarter of all government spending, and education had fallen to fourth place, at a little over 10 per cent. The significance of such changes is self-evident: we may look upon education as an investment in the young, in the ability of the "new ones," as the Greeks called them, to innovate, to initiate, to act. Much, of course, will depend on what they are taught, but that is another question. The point is that a society that chooses education over welfare is investing in the potential for success rather than the certainty of failure. Of course, there can be no certainty of success, and not all who fail wish everyone else to join them. Perhaps it just looks that way when the welfare state has become a dinosaur.

After the vast increase in welfare expenditures, the other great change has been the percentage of government expenditures that goes to provide no services at all. These dollars are used to pay for last year's services that were paid for at the time by borrowing. In 1970 around 9 cents of every expenditure dollar was for interest payments; by 1988 it was nearly 19 cents. Today it is around 30 cents.

Why is this rise in the national debt and the attendant decline in discretionary expenditures significant? One way to look at debt is to consider it as deferred tax. And those who will pay it are future generations. It is, in a sense, a perfect crime because the victims are too young to do anything about it now (or are as yet unborn) and when they are old enough to seek justice, the perpetrators will fast be disappearing. This has the same effect as funding welfare or medicare through education cutbacks: in both cases the young suffer. More obviously, the growth of the debt is evidence that older Canadians believe that the inability to pay should not bar them from having what they want now. And yet there is surely something amiss when we pay out of empty pockets. An old Spanish proverb comes to mind: "Take what you want," said God; "Take it and pay for it." One is also reminded of the TV ad: "You can pay me now or pay me later." The meaning of both seems clear enough: when we try to pay for things by enlarging our debts, things are bound to end in tears. It surely makes matters worse when the old pay for their own toys by using the credit cards of their children.

To get a truer overall picture of what went wrong, however, we need to look beyond the fact that nearly a third of government spending is for debt servicing, which is not optional or discretionary. If you ignore interest payments and look only at the way governments have allocated *discretionary* money, the increase in social welfare expenditures looms even larger. In 1970, education and social welfare each took about 20 per cent of expenditures; by 1988, education had fallen by 7 per cent and social welfare had increased by about the same amount. In per capita terms, excluding interest on the accumulated debt and adjusting for inflation, governments have more than doubled per capita expenditures during this period. The significance of the choice of social welfare over education is clear enough: Canadians or their governments have chosen to invest in protecting those who seem to have become incapable of helping themselves, rather than in training the young so they will become capable of helping themselves. Here is truly the dead hand of the past.

The other significant change, in health costs (up from under $200 per capita in 1970 to more than $1,400 by 1988), indicates another dimension beyond the sheer increase in communitarian tendencies. Health care is part of the service sector of the economy. Because sick bodies tend to stay home and because only doctors and other "health practitioners" are permitted to provide this service, health care is better insulated from foreign competition than the rest of the service sector. That is why doctors are so well paid and, except at the very high end, there is no cross-border shopping. Best of all, the market can never be saturated because we all must die. Not surprisingly, costs rise wonderfully during the last few months, weeks, hours, and even minutes of life. There will, accordingly, always be a demand for more health care — a demand that will continue to increase as long as those who receive treatment do not have to pay for it directly.

Two things are especially perverse in health care, which should properly be called "sickness care." The first is that it is an extreme form of the perfect crime, since it must be paid for even when the patient dies. The second is that increased costs of uncompetitive health care can look like growth in the GDP because more jobs are created. We can see, however, just what each job so created is really worth when we ask the common-sense question: "Do we create more wealth by getting sicker and paying one another for our own care?"

The continuing momentum that drives public expenditure is clear: while the demand for health and social welfare services is expanding, we are unwilling to pay for them. Moreover, the recent record indicates that it is very difficult to distinguish a high-spending from a low-spending party. It can be done, of course, and the Liberals turn out to be bigger spenders than the Conservatives — but not by much. Nearly everyone agrees that it is desirable to provide more health and welfare services, and debate centres on the rate of increase or the impact that an increase may have on the debt. This agreement, we submit, is evidence that collectivist opinions are now widely accepted as authoritative guides to formulating public policy. In fact, the degree to which one espouses collectivism is the measure of one's political correctness. To determine how politically correct you are, ask yourself whether you consider it cruel and uncaring even to raise the question of cost with respect to the sick, the injured, and the dying. Moralizing collectivists, brimming over with indignation, are sure to charge us with insensitivity at best — and more likely with barbaric cruelty — for even considering such issues. "What would you do," they cry, "shut down hospitals?" The clever among them would say: "Well, what do you expect? They are from Alberta. They do unspeakable things like that out there." And yet, the facts remain: spending lots of money on sickness care disproportionately benefits the old, not the young. And since no one gets out alive, it seems perfectly legitimate to question the investment strategy and call to account the collectivist doctrine that justifies our priorities. As we all know, the accounts do not look good.

Another way to see the perversity of the welfare state is to consider directly its governing assumption, that society is more like a machine than an organism. Parts can be changed around and you can test whether the new configuration works better, or, if it doesn't work better, at least looks nicer. It is rather like rearranging the furniture in the den: Do I want the TV over there by the window, or next to the CD player? Do I want the government or a Crown corporation to deliver the mail or provide garbage collection or should I turn that business over to business? We would probably be a lot less sanguine about government intervention if we dropped such mechanical imagery. If we think of society as an organic entity we can more easily see the consequences: Do I want a kidney there in my middle or next to my ear? Would I prefer to have two left feet or a third eye?

With or without the imagery, the point is obvious: all action induces suffering, an insight one learns from Homer. So when the government acts on society or intervenes in any way, it induces suffering. Usually we call this "social costs" or "transaction costs" or "unanticipated consequences." Or, to return to the difference between rearranging TV sets and easy chairs or kidneys and feet, it is clear that, in trying to change complex and interdependent things, such as human bodies or society (or the economy), it is much easier to botch the job than to improve on what is there. A butcher can easily rearrange body parts in immediately lethal ways, but how many skilled surgeons can actually improve upon what (vital if imperfect) nature has provided?

There are other perversities as well. The logic of the welfare state, directed towards ensuring that there are no losers, leads to the conclusion that to be a victim is to be a winner. When losers appear on the scene, as inevitably they do, it is not politically correct to suggest that they have lost fair and square or to decry them in any way. Rather, the "correct" position is that they are entitled to win, and so are "really" winners. And to prove it, they deserve and get help. They deserve help because charity is "demeaning" if accepted and insulting if offered. Thus, the old social virtue of liberality becomes impossible.

There is, however, one exception, which it is politically incorrect even to mention: biological reproduction. Since the early nineteenth century, birth rates have varied inversely with income: the rich have barely reproduced themselves. Never until now, however, have certain cultural groups (such as Native people) been able to sustain more offspring than they could support from their own resources. For the first time in thousands of generations it is possible for an underclass to be the most rapidly growing sector of the population. The point of this observation is not to criticize the very poor, whether Native or not, but to draw attention to a bizarre instance of the perversity of communitarianism: economic failure and victimhood have become a successful strategy for cultural as well as biological reproduction. But whatever causes the development of an underclass, whether in Canada or elsewhere, it seems clear that the behaviour of people who find themselves in such a position today does not lead to the development of skills, to economic success, or to pride in one's contribution to the country as a whole.

Public Employment

A second indicator of the growth of collectivism is an increase in public employment. The link between the two is that an increase in government activity entails an increase in its labour force. The relationship is not necessarily directly proportionate, since government employees are not notoriously efficient, but an increase in the size of the government workforce does have the advantage of accurately reflecting the growth in the public use of real economic resources. We will focus our concern on the federal public service, though there is no doubt that similar trends can be found in the other two orders of government as well.

At two separate moments in our history, the civil service has approximately doubled over the course of a decade. The first time was between the early 1940s and the early 1950s; the second time was between 1965 and 1975. After the end of World War Two, the civil service expanded to absorb military veterans (overwhelmingly men); after 1965, it expanded to absorb the baby boomers they sired. The greatest difference, however, was that in 1945 the former soldiers generally brought with them the attitudes of enlisted men, attitudes that enabled them to adapt easily to the quasi-military structure that characterized the postwar bureaucracy. The boomers, male and female, on the other hand, were mostly university graduates and entered, so to speak, with the attitudes of freshly minted general officers. They had no direct experience of the world, but they were bursting with a desire to improve it, chiefly through state action. In the words of Ian Tyson, their dreams have lost some grandeur coming true, and today we all must put up with the results of the second wave, namely great overrepresentation of headquarters staff, especially of male, middle-aged middle managers who have nowhere to go and not much worth doing.

In fact, the postwar expansion was proportionately greater than that of the 1960s, but it was relatively trouble-free, "a tidal wave without a storm," as one observer said. There were several reasons for this. First, fear of a return to the hungry thirties after wartime expansion meant that the increase was both prudent and defensive. Most of the new civil servants, for example, were classified as temporary, which meant that most of the new jobs were at the bottom of the pay scale. Indeed, there were more temporary positions in the civil service than permanent ones until 1960. Moreover, the expansion took place across the entire country — in the Post Office, for example. The boomer expansion took place almost entirely in Ottawa. And lastly, the postwar cohort had known both economic depression and war before they entered the labour market. Their expectations were accordingly modest, their personal habits were frugal, and they were accustomed to order and hierarchy. None of this was true of the boomers. On the contrary, their expectations were grandiose, they had never known anything but prosperity and economic expansion, and they greatly admired the experiences of participatory democracy.

In many ways, as Mitchell Sharp's recent memoirs vividly attest, the postwar era was the golden age of mandarins. Both politicians and the public accepted their power because everyone had confidence in the mandarins' expertise and ability. The mandarins reciprocated by showing themselves deserving of public trust. Promotions were rare, so the security of the men (and they were nearly all male) at the top was unchallenged by Young Turks or rising stars. The "Ottawa men," as J.L. Granatstein called them, saw public service as a vocation not a profession or a career. Lower civil servants, the vast pool of "temporary" employees, could expect but one promotion during their entire period of employment, and those who joined late in life, including many of the veterans, could count on retiring at the same level at which they had entered. Interdepartmental mobility was minimal. In short, the postwar civil service was "Japanese" in its management practices:

security was traded for paternalism and rigidity. Expertise was born of experience.

Despite the apparent competence of the civil service, however, ominous changes were already under way by the late 1940s. From the point of view of the government of the day, the reliability of the civil service looked more like stubborn inflexibility. According to the mandarins, the best way of doing things was the way it was being done. Some of them even proclaimed their ways to be the necessary way, which meant that changes were next to impossible; but the politicians were eager for change. Moreover, Young Turks, eyes burning with the truth of Keynesian economics, were ready to transform the government into an agent of social and economic change. The government would, they said, generate employment opportunities that, in turn, could be administered as new government ventures.

A brief look at the purpose of modern economics may show the significance of this new approach. From its inception in the seventeenth century, economics has sought to provide a substitute for virtue. As we shall see, however, there are no free moral lunches. The new economic science promised not just to make us better off, but to make us better people. The doctrine that the early economists attacked and that contemporary economists scorn was expressed beautifully in the fable of the ant and the grasshopper. The more direct language that was used before economics and the assumptions of economists set the agenda said: "Do not put all your faith in good times because bad times are sure to follow; when they do you will be sorry, and it will be too late. Emulate the ant and put aside for a rainy day and a cold winter. Grasshoppers who spend the happy days of summer frolicking and singing are fools." In other words, don't rely on fortune, whether good fortune or bad, because fortune is unreliable. You really never know. Instead, the wisdom that predates economics instructs us to rely on virtue and on the traditions that secure virtue. Nowadays, it is a rare individual who will even acknowledge the existence of virtue, let alone propose that there are ways to secure it. Economists have done their bit to produce our present circumstances. They have rightly insisted that there is no such thing as a free lunch: scarce resources have a cost. They wished, however, to exclude moral costs from the equation, and that was a big mistake.

In the days prior to economics, good and bad times were understood to be irremediable. Economics transformed the alternation of good and bad times into the business cycle. Suddenly, responsibility could be assigned for what had previously been understood as the natural dearth or divine retribution of the seven lean years; scarcity was now understood to be the consequence of human action and responses. And these merely human things could be predicted, anticipated, and altered. Armed with this new scientific economic knowledge, governments could limit the amplitude of the business cycle and redeem the promise to "improve the lot" of people whose lot otherwise would have been left to fortune. Pre-Keynesian economics described the autonomous operation of the market, where autonomy meant "free from political determination or interference." This pre-Keynesian doctrine appealed greatly to liberals because it transformed the notion of virtue, which had previously been determined by the state, or perhaps the church, by equating it with unsupervised freedom. The rewards of virtue could now be reaped by those with a spirit of independence unguided by authority, tradition, or habit. Liberals would be led by reason. Not full philosophical reason, perhaps, but at least led by reasoned calculations.

Keynes revised this doctrine so that economists could take control not of an autonomous system but of an economy that could be tended in such a way that full employment and endless prosperity would result. "Tending" the economy meant that governments would not leave the economy alone but, on the contrary, would manipulate demand through expenditures from the public purse.

In passing, we might make the observation that proponents of the recent fashion for "supply-side economics" did not call into question the governing assumption of the Keynesians. Theirs was an intramural spat. The difference between the two sides lay in the recommendation of the supply-siders that the appropriate "intervention" was a tax cut. Either way, they were still economists and, so, devoted to the doctrine that governments are wholly or partially responsible for controlling the business cycle. But as we shall see in detail in the chapters that follow, governments have proved themselves incapable of exercising that responsibility. On the contrary, their interventions have simply added one more uncontrollable element to our collective life, including the business cycle.

One conclusion we may draw is that economics is less a quantitative science like biochemistry or civil engineering than a moral science. If this is so, and we think it is, then it would obviously have been more prudent to consider the succession of good times and bad to be irremediable. Why? Because if it turns out that government intervention, undertaken to influence or control the so-called business cycle, in fact ensures that the succession of good times and bad becomes irremediable, then we will, in fact, be worse off. Why? Because we will be unable to grasp why the analyses and conclusions of the economists have failed. In Canada today we have reached the point where the Great Crash and Depression of Keynesian economics has taken place, but no one wants to admit it because no one knows what to put in its place. And yet, it has collapsed. The Great Crash of Keynesianism is evident in the complete, utter and obvious failure of all the social programs devised by government to deal with the deficiencies of an "untended" economy. The Depression that followed the Crash is still with us insofar as Canadians have expectations that Keynesianism has stimulated but cannot satisfy. The evidence is present in our daily newspapers: expenditures by governments must be reduced, but cuts in services are intolerable. Once Canadians learned to eat free lunches, including the free moral lunches served up by economists of every stripe, then, human nature being what it is, they became reluctant to pay for them. Do any of us really see ourselves as kind, generous, and willing taxpayers? Who among us wishes to pay today for yesterday's unnecessary services that were delivered to somebody else whom we don't much like or admire anyhow?

In his splendid book, *America's Constitutional Soul*, Harvey Mansfield has drawn our attention to another, less obvious conclusion: if we are going to rely on the market to deliver the goods we must be satisfied with the goods it delivers. We may have certain expectations, and we may position ourselves to take advantage of certain opportunities as they arise, but we cannot demand certain results, such as full, or near-full, or indeed any specific level of employment. The reason is simple: if we do, we change the nature of employment. You are not, properly speaking, employed unless you can be unemployed as well. To have a job you must have a boss; and a boss can fire you. If the government guarantees you a job, Mansfield said, "it becomes something like a professorship," a tenured professorship at that, with no teaching, research, or administrative responsibilities for the non-performance of which one could be fired. And then, as the recent experiences of Central European socialism have shown the world, "the economy descends to the productivity of a university, and society becomes as ill-natured as an academic community that is not supported by a buoyant economy." All Canadian academics know how friendly universities have become lately.

Notwithstanding the intention of economics to supply us with a substitute for virtue, there is nevertheless a moral bottom line to Keynesian as well as to pre- and post-Keynesian economics, revealed by the question "How does this doctrine recommend we behave? As borrowers and spenders, or as workers and savers? As grasshoppers or as ants?" The answer will promote certain kinds of behaviour and certain kinds of character, and demote others. Borrowers and spenders do well when there is inflation; workers and savers benefit when prices remain steady. Inevitably, then, we are returned to the question of virtue: Is it better to live by one's own efforts as worker and saver than to be better off by borrowing and spending other people's money? And what if the "other people" are one's children, who will eventually have to pay the taxes we now defer as debt? When the question is posed that way, the indignation experienced by liberals at the follies of the collectivists is not only intelligible but righteous.

When we look at the origins of the boomers' bureaucracy, it is hard not to sympathize with the liberals' indignation. The boomers discovered a need to use the public service, as it had come to be known, as a "social safety valve." Unlike the men of 1945, however, the children of the 1960s had none of the clarity of purpose and discipline of the vets. Instead, they sought to expand the field of government intervention. They had bright ideas and lots of energy and were armed with a purpose: to transform a mere bureaucratic organization into an active government.

For those involved in the "new task," job satisfaction must have been very high. In America, the best and the brightest, as David Halberstam called them, undertook exhilarating nation building in

Southeast Asia; in Canada they felt they were being even more useful by building a just society at home, without air strikes or search-and-destroy missions. They were well paid to build, without violence, a nation in which people would have better health and be better housed and better educated than ever before. It looked as if dreams could come true with their grandeur intact.

In 1960, for example, soon-to-be Prime Minister Lester B. Pearson issued a manifesto that promised to address "regional disparities," to revamp manpower policies, and to reform social services. The most impressive result was a 54 per cent growth in the size of the bureaucracy over the next eight years. In 1966 medicare was instituted. A year later collective bargaining for federal employees was allowed. No longer were civil servants soldiers without uniforms; now they were Canadian workers. Unlike other Canadian workers, however, they shared none of the exposure of real workers to the possibility of economic bad times. Even more than academics, civil servants have tenure. In many respects they live in a society without real risks. But the initiatives came from the politicians. As we shall see, new departments were created out of thin air: Forestry in 1960; Industry in 1963; Consumer Affairs in 1966.

In 1960 the Glassco Commission (on Government Services), which had been appointed by Prime Minister John Diefenbaker, issued its report. Its most famous recommendation or slogan was: "Management to the Manager." This meant that financial controls would be eased. The old watchdog, Treasury Board, became a coordinator, not a controller. If new programs could be justified on policy grounds, departments were free to increase spending. Although Glassco also recommended an independent review procedure outside the bureaucracy to oversee the newly unleashed managers, that recommendation was somehow ignored. So the higher echelons of the bureaucracy put their imaginations to work and found new ways to advance their own careers. In 1952, for example, promotions were 14 per cent of all appointments; by 1970 promotions were 34 per cent. Promotions meant higher salaries for those who were promoted, of course; but it also ensured that the new recruits, the rising stars who flew up to the commanding heights, were guaranteed to be inexperienced in management. Glassco thought that letting managers manage was a recipe for administrative competence, but only because he assumed that the new managers knew how to manage. He was, to say the least, too sanguine.

We will examine some of the more outrageous examples of bureaucratic collectivism in chapter 4. It is, perhaps, sufficient to note here that it has been estimated that the administrative staff of the bureaucracy has grown by a factor of ten since the end of World War Two, whereas the whole bureaucratic apparatus has grown to merely four times its immediate postwar size. It would be difficult to find or invent a more perfect example of Parkinson's Law.

Special Status

A third indicator of the impact of collectivist doctrines can be found in the series of constitutional fiascos with which Canadians have lacerated themselves. In a previous book, *Deconfederation: Canada Without Quebec*, we discussed in detail the origins of the Quebec question, and we offered a solution to it. It might have worked, but history is strewn with untried proposals for what might have been. The French of Quebec have to date shown that they are not willing to leave Canada; Canadians are, for their part, unwilling even to consider the possibility of expelling Quebec. An opportunity, perhaps for greatness, has been lost. However that may be, it seems self-evident that the continuing demands by successive Quebec governments, and now by Quebec MPs sitting as the Bloc Québécois, are collectivist in nature. The topic will recur in the course of this account of what went wrong, so only the briefest indication needs to be made in the present context.

As we argued earlier, one of the fundamental principles of liberal democratic government is the equality of individuals before the law. According to this principle, there are no officially second-class citizens, and no legally privileged aristocrats who could be judged only by their aristocratic peers. Collectivism challenges this principle, as we noted earlier in this chapter. Demands for collective rights also lead to conflicts between or among collectivities. For example, both the Government of Quebec and the James Bay Cree have advanced arguments in defence of their interests that are based on ill-considered notions of collective rights. The resulting round of mutual recrimination testifies to the wisdom of liberal individualism.

We do not wish to be misunderstood. To favour liberal individualism is not to deny the importance of groups and collectivities in liberal democracies. After all, freedom of association is an important component of individual freedom. The question is not whether one is for or against groups and collectivities but whether and to what extent they should be given legal and constitutional status and recognition — especially since we know from long experience that special legal status for some groups will always generate ill-will among others; it is not a recipe for comity among one's fellow citizens.

Many of those opposed to the Meech Lake Accord, for example, rejected special status for Quebec. No one denied that in some respects Quebec is a distinct society, but for many it did not follow that Canada should have two classes of citizens, those under the jurisdiction of the Government of Quebec and everyone else. In particular, Native leaders, including Elijah Harper, whose activities in the Manitoba Legislature ensured the defeat of the Accord, argued that if there was ever a distinct society that deserved special legal status, it was the Aboriginal inhabitants of Canada.

Aboriginal peoples, of course, already have special legal status. But they are largely unhappy with it. While nearly everyone considers the Indian Act to be unsatisfactory, Native people are reluctant to abandon it. On the one hand, they rightly consider the antiquated paternalism of the Act to be an affront to their dignity. No one likes to be a servile pensioner. As we shall see, however, we have all become pensioners of a sort, so that the question of collective rights for Native people throws other questions into sharp relief as well. One solution that has been proposed is to grant Native communities self-government. In the language favoured by spokespersons for the Native "community," the Government of Canada and, one assumes, Canadian citizens, are invited to acknowledge that Aboriginal peoples have an inherent right of self-government. The current minister has indicated that, until the courts rule otherwise, he intends to formulate policy on the basis of that inherent right. One might raise at least one question regarding Native self-government: would it undermine the obligations of the federal government, especially its financial obligations?

The inherent difficulties in the inherent right to self-government are, in fact, much deeper than the question of who pays for it. Self-government is a political manifestation of self-determination. On the one hand, it is the most visible kind of self-determination, since it implies legitimacy and support, external recognition of internal authority, and adequate resources to enable that authority to enforce its decisions. No self-governing body can be made up of pensioners dependent upon others, no matter what the alleged moral obligation may be to provide the dependants with handouts. On the other hand, a community concerned with self-determination can determine to avoid self-government and be content to rely on handouts from others while insisting upon its autonomy from their control in some areas. In fact, most Native leaders appear to be confused on the distinction: by the inherent right to self-government they seem to mean limited self-determination. And who sets the limits constitutes the substance of negotiation. To put it bluntly, Native leaders will play the "inherent right" card in order to extract as large a payment as possible from the so-called colonizers, namely Canadian taxpayers. But they really can have no right to self-government while remaining pensioners. This is not a hard-hearted observation that betrays our lack of a generous spirit; it follows from the inherent logic of self-government. That is, self-government must be based on economic self-sufficiency or else it turns into the fraudulent whining for more cash. It is fraudulent because Canadians do not owe Native people anything. It is whining because any putatively self-respecting Native person knows this and is ashamed at having to give up his or her self-respect in order to make a claim on somebody else's money.

The same problem has arisen in connection with the Quebec question, so it is nothing new to Canadian political observers. Premier Bourassa's famous doctrine of *fédéralisme rentable*, profitable federalism, contained the same underhanded attempt to get something for nothing — the joys of self-determination without the obligations of self-government or the demands of economic self-sufficiency. As we said in *Deconfederation*, it was unacceptable for Quebec to assume such a position *vis-à-vis* Canada, and the same thing is true with respect to Native people. Regardless of how the problem is resolved, the Native view is that the solution must enhance rather than diminish their special legal status. Native people and Quebec nationalists thus share a common premise. But it has done little to create harmony between them. *Au contraire!*

The clash of interests between the two groups was brought into sharp focus by the conflict over the second phase of the mammoth James Bay hydroelectric development. Native objections to this project are by no means limited to the claim that they are being denied their fair share of the prosperity it will supposedly bring. More significantly, the James Bay Cree claim the project would destroy their way of life, which, they say, they have a right to defend. Here again their argument parallels that of Quebec nationalists. Both Native people and Quebec nationalists base their claims on an argument of principle formulated in the language of rights. Historically, the language of rights was developed in Europe as part of the liberal strategic plan to dethrone the claim that certain types or classes of people — namely, aristocrats and priests — had a natural or revealed right to rule. That is, the language of rights was developed to defend individuals against the tyrannical pretensions of groups, and against the civil strife that was inevitably produced by contested group-based claims to rule. By nature, liberals said, individuals have the right to be governed with their own consent, and are entitled to rebel against governments that ignore that consent. The reason for the centrality of consent in liberal democracy is obvious, though perhaps it bears repeating. It is the right that joins all other rights to government because it makes clear that the purpose of government is to secure rights, not to create them. Accordingly, rights do not exist at or for the convenience of government. Put negatively, if governments are understood to be capable of creating rights without seeking the consent of the governed, then they can just as easily remove them, also without consent. This is why Native groups declare or claim that their right to self-government is inherent and, so, capable of recognition. It does not, they maintain, need to be created by statutory or constitutional law. With respect to the James Bay question, the Cree might argue that Quebec governs them without their consent. Of course, they are outvoted, but that is not what they mean. Rather they object that the Cree way of life is systematically excluded from consideration by the Québécois. They have a point, of course, but what is it?

Richard Le Hir, chairman of the Coalition for Great Whale and vice-president of the Quebec Manufacturers Association, declared that a marginal group of a few hundred Natives should not be allowed to stop a project that is clearly in the interests of millions of Quebeckers. Fernand Daoust, president of the Quebec Federation of Labour agreed: 90,000 jobs were at stake. Michel Yergeau, a lawyer for Hydro Quebec, said that involving the federal government merely because it had a constitutional obligation to protect the interests of Native people was "rubbish." It would unfairly block Quebec's economic development. That similar arguments might with equal justification be used by the Canadian majority against the nationalist claims of the Quebec minority apparently escaped the notice of these Québécois spokesmen. The doctrine "what is sauce for the goose is sauce for the gander" never holds much appeal for geese who wish to have nothing to do with ganders.

For their part, Native leaders have responded in kind. When Premier Bourassa criticized Elijah Harper as an enemy of national unity, Ovide Mercredi, national chief of the Assembly of First Nations, claimed this was an attack on "all the Aboriginal people, the original inhabitants of this country." One is reminded here of Premier Bourassa's claim that the defeat of Meech Lake was a collective humiliation, an insult to all Quebeckers, by which he meant all French Quebeckers. Additional parallels exist as well. After the "insult" of the Meech Lake failure, the Quebec government proposed a future referendum to prepare for secession from Canada. Not surprisingly, Chief Billy Diamond of Waskaganish declared that the James Bay deal of 1975 would be dead if Quebec left Canada. Upon separation, he said, the Cree would retain the territory extended to Quebec in 1898 and 1912. He, too, would prepare to establish a new state. His colleague, Grand Chief Matthew Coon Come, added that this new state would be unilingual — unilingual Cree.

Both groups — French Quebeckers after Meech Lake, the James Bay Cree later on — are assuming that collective rights have been violated. Because of this violation, it is necessary to obtain territory separate from that of the violators, Canada and Quebec. To date, however, we have seen merely threats, closely followed by proposals to avoid separation. We all know the game being played by Quebec: the Liberals, provincial and federal, are the good cops; the Parti Québécois and the Bloc Québécois are the bad cops. But if French Quebec can play that game against Canada, why can't the Cree play the same way against Quebec?

Speaking to the Cree of northern Quebec, Ovide Mercredi proposed a highly decentralized Canada as the solution to all our difficulties. The First Nations, he said should have all the powers presently being sought by the Province of Quebec. Like Quebec, they must have greater control over natural resources. The similarity between his position and that of the Premier of Quebec was not lost on him. Mr. Bourassa was, so to speak, an objective ally. It was much to be regretted, Mr. Mercredi allowed, that he was "not acting like one."

It is here that we confront the dilemma of advocating collective rights. Membership has its privileges, to be sure, but why should non-members have the slightest interest in recognizing them? When collectivities and not individuals become the bearers of rights, it is hard to avoid the conclusion that the only way they can relate to one another is, as René Lévesque said of Canada and Quebec, like two scorpions in a bottle.

It seems to us that Lévesque had a point. So do Ovide Mercredi, Matthew Coon Come, and Jacques Parizeau. But again, what is it? In our view, it is the heart of the problem of collectivist politics — the assertion of group rights. And in Canada today, group rights are asserted by many more collectivities than Native people and French Quebeckers. The principle for disruption can be summarized as follows: when groups based on such characteristics as race, ethnicity, culture, or gender are given explicit constitutional status, they inevitably compare their status to that of other groups, ever vigilant for evidence of inequity. What is given to one group is resented by others, giving rise to an unending search for enhanced constitutional status.

The dynamics were played out during the twilight period between the failure of the Meech Lake Accord and the repudiation of the Charlottetown Accord. The Government of Canada apparently was of the opinion that group rights were an important part of what it means to be a Canadian. The first clause of the pre-Charlottetown "package" declared group rights to be essential to "the Canadian experience…. The fact that community rights exist alongside individual rights in our Constitution goes to the heart of what Canada is about." We can see the problem explicitly in the short-lived proposal to give Native people guaranteed seats in the Senate. The government itself seemed to recognize there was a difficulty because, while it also wished to promote the increased representation of "women, visible minorities, language groups, and the disabled" in the Senate, it did not propose to give any of these groups guaranteed representation. That privilege was reserved for Aboriginals. But some feminists quickly demanded similar treatment for women. Once the principle of guaranteed group representation is granted, how can other groups be excluded from its benefits? But when representation is allocated by group what happens to electoral freedom? The answer is not to grant the principle. The government, or rather the bright minds from certain political science departments (which, in the interests of professional courtesy, if not of justice, must remain unnamed), seemed to think that group representation of this kind was analogous to guaranteed territorial representation in the Senate. But the analogy is highly strained. Among other things, one can move in and out of territories, but one cannot readily change one's race, ethnicity, or gender.

In our view, Canadians have been led, perhaps unwittingly, towards impossible collectivist goals. Because those goals are impossible and can never be achieved, government attempts to achieve them simply make matters worse. Expectations have been raised that can never be met.

In the pages that follow we will indicate in detail not just what went wrong but how. As Frank McKenna said after the Meech Lake fiasco, there is plenty of blame to go around. But our purpose here is not to apportion blame. Rather, it is to impart whatever understanding we can. In this chapter we have suggested that the first thing to understand is that our current modes and orders are perverse. By raising expectations far beyond the possibility of meeting them we have created the causes of our own frustration. But we do not need to continue in our perversity. We are not compelled to inflate our expectations in order to savour the bilious taste of defeat. We need not be a nation of whiners, stinking with self-righteousness and resentment.

How do we know this? Because there was a time when Canadians did not demand things that no government could provide. There was a time when Canadians and their governments knew that it was essential to balance demands and resources. The harsh face of necessity has not gone away, though we have become fearful of gazing upon it. Once Canadians knew that the only way to deal with fortune, particularly malign fortune, was with virtue. Once Canadian political leaders knew that the chief political virtue was moderation. In the vivid language of the Psalmist, we have become defiled with our own words and have gone a-whoring with our own inventions. And as with the ancient Israelites, we chose that course. No one compelled us to take it. It is for that reason as well that Canadians are both responsible for the mess they have made and are capable of ending it. In the following chapter we will see what good government once was in Canada. Then follows the sorry tale of woe. We conclude by indicating not so much how to restore good government as what policies might allow its recovery.

2
What Good Government Meant

et us begin at the beginning. July 1, 1867, fell on a Monday; it was the start of a new week, a new month, and a new nation — Canada. But what kind of a nation was it to be? Ontario's George Brown, one of the most important Fathers of Confederation, had no doubts. His Toronto *Globe* proclaimed: "With the first dawn of this gladsome midsummer morn, we hail this birthday of a new nationality. A united British America, with its four millions of people, takes its place this day among the nations of the world ... this day a new volume is opened." For Brown, but also for his political opponent, Sir John A. Macdonald, and for Macdonald's ally, Sir George-Etienne Cartier, the great attraction of the new nationality was the promise of greater prosperity.

When we consider the shape that Canada's finances are now in — its people have never been more heavily taxed and rarely as sorely tried economically — it is a sad irony that Canada is one of the few nations on the face of the globe to have been founded primarily to improve the economic well-being of its inhabitants. Most modern nations were established to give expression to the ethnic, cultural, religious, or even regional aspirations of some definable group of people. It is true that the founding of the United States promised to enhance the economic opportunities of its people, but unlike the founding of Canada, the birth of the United States, from the Declaration of Independence in 1776 to the adoption of the Constitution in 1787–89, was also intended to put into practice a set of widely held political and philosophical principles. These principles had been developing within the Thirteen Colonies for more than 100 years prior to the American Revolution.

In the British American colonies of the mid-1860s, there were few, if any, political philosophers. In the realm of political ideas, Victorian platitudes about the greatness of the Empire and constitutional monarchy prevailed, not well thought out political arguments or deep reflections on political principles. Even if Canada had been awash in political philosophers, the search for political and philosophical principles to govern the relations of citizens to each other and to their government was probably the farthest thing from the minds of such practical-minded politicians as John A. Macdonald. He and the other Fathers of Confederation had very real problems to resolve, and quickly, lest their cherished British American way of life disappear. The government of pre-Confederation Canada (consisting of Canada West, or Ontario, and Canada East, or Quebec) had been virtually deadlocked for years; the credit of all the British North American colonies had nearly been exhausted; the impending expiry of the Reciprocity Treaty with the United States, signed in 1854, was about to put serious obstacles in the way of the already significant north-south trade flow; the Americans were truculent, angry with Britain for backing the South in the Civil War and apparently ready to march north against Canada.

Macdonald and the others already took for granted that constitutional monarchy, with its sovereignty vested in the Crown, and the British system of the orderly rule of law to sustain individual liberty were far superior to what they thought of as American "mobocracy." They did not create, nor did they want to create, a new constitutional or political entity to express some new constitutional way of ordering the political world. Their aims, then, were far less lofty than those of the founders of the "Great Republic" to the south. They had no aspirations to inaugurate a *novus ordo seclorum*, a new order of the ages, as the Americans boldly proclaim on their greenbacks. The Fathers of Confederation wanted greater security, more trade opportunities, a reorganized public debt, and the creation of a central British North American government charged with the task, and provided with the legislative tools, to foster economic growth. For the balance of this book we will call those aims economic fundamentalism — the belief that good government and the Canadian nation must rest on a solid economic foundation and that *a* chief, if not *the* chief purpose of government is to secure the conditions for prosperity.

No matter how Macdonald and the other leaders of Canada twisted and turned, union of the British American colonies seemed the only way to restore their credit rating, end the deadlock in the Canadian government, broaden their markets, and allow them some semblance of a chance of defending themselves militarily against the United States. But in the face of the great linguistic, religious, and ethnic cleavage between the French-speaking and the English-speaking peoples, and the no less important divisions of religion, region, and ethnicity among the English-speaking British Americans themselves, how could such a union be sustained? That was the supreme challenge facing the Fathers of Confederation.

For George Brown, as for other founders of Canada, the new "nation" they were building had to be very different from the national states of Europe. First of all, the European states owed their existence to the seventeenth-century wars of religion. They persisted in the context of a European "balance of power" and began to disintegrate with the tremendous nineteenth-century overseas expansion of Britain, France, and Germany, as well as with the increasing importance of the United States. This does not mean, of course, that the formal and legal definition of a state could not be extended from its original home in Europe to cover multinational empires such as Russia's or new regimes such as the American. In fact, however, the United States and Canada were never states in the European sense. The United States was a republic and a federation, and Canada, of course, was a dominion, which was also something other than a state in the European sense.

Historically, there is another complication that should be kept in mind if we are properly to appreciate the uniqueness of the establishment of Canada. The European state system of the eighteenth and nineteenth centuries was also by and large a system of national states. A state is a legal reality: it is an internally obeyed and externally recognized legal thing. A nation is a cultural reality, not a legal one. Like states, nations are European. Properly speaking, they do not exist in America, Africa, or Asia; nor can they be found in Antarctica, Australia, or Oceania. Nations came into existence when peoples acquired a consciousness of themselves as cultural and historical entities. There was more to nationality in this strict European sense than a sense of a common culture. Nations were also conscious of their territory as a permanent home, where history — their labours and their wars, their city building and road and wall building — had left visible traces. Cultivation of the homeland was the common labour of their ancestors; and its future would depend upon the transmission of a common and particular civilization.

Historically speaking, whenever nation states came into being immigration ceased. This meant that peasants, agricultural workers firmly tied to the national soil, were a prerequisite for a genuine nationality. To be more precise, nations are not so much made up of peasants as of ex-peasants, peasants who have achieved political emancipation and gone on to take control of the state from the former monarchs and aristocrats.

States, as we said, were legal structures. All persons who live in states are circumscribed by laws, either in the sense that laws protect their rights, or in the sense that laws oppress them. In either case, what people could or could not do was determined by law. Most importantly, as a supreme legal structure the state protected (or oppressed) all who lived under its aegis regardless of national, religious, ethnic, or linguistic status. It was a growth in national consciousness that altered the legal structure of the state. In the name of the people — that is, of the nation — the state was forced to recognize as citizens only nationals. That is, in Europe, only nationals were full citizens; only nationals had full political and civil rights by virtue of their origin and fact of birth. Non-nationals had to be protected by special laws or else they were oppressed — as nationals, but foreign nationals this time.

There is a final historical complication to consider regarding the European nation state. Without going too far afield into historical detail, one can say that the same process that brought about the decline of monarchy as the sole expression of sovereignty brought about the existence of classes. With the end of monarchy and the growth of popular sovereignty, the common interest, which the king had once upon a time represented, was in danger of dissolving into conflicting class interests — a recipe for permanent civil war. The only bond remaining to the citizens of a nation state without a monarch to symbolize their common interest was (or seemed to be) common national origin. From the start of the historical evolution of the European nation state, therefore, there has been a conflict between universal legal rights and particular collective national rights. This conflict, we shall see, also appeared in Canada when, eventually, Canadians were forced to think about the legal structure of their polity. In Europe, however, the practical outcome was that legal rights, the rights guaranteed by the state, were protected and enforced only as national rights. In the strict sense, nationalism can be understood as the subordination of the state to the nation and the identification of the citizen and the national.

There are, of course, derivative ways of using the terms "nation" and "state." Cartier, to give an obvious Canadian example, spoke of the new country as a "political nation," as distinct, in his mind, from the ethnic, cultural, linguistic, or religiously homogeneous nations of Europe. The point of this brief digression into European political history is simply this: where the trinity of people, territory, and state does not exist, there cannot be nation states either. The words can, however, be used in a derivative and strategic way. Many peoples want to be nations because being a nation is seen to be sufficient to acquire a state. In Canada we speak easily of "First Nations," and the legislature of Quebec is called the National Assembly. The purpose of this strategic self-identification of collectives as nations is to ensure that the state or, more generally, political authority is to be subordinate to the nation. What the aspirants for national status want, by and large, is independence, prestige, recognition — in other words, power and collective visibility. They are not chiefly concerned with creating a legal state structure for all citizens but rather with using the law to protect and defend what they identify with the nation.

As we will see in detail in the chapters that follow, this derivative form of nation has come to constitute a major stumbling block in Canadian politics. Indeed, confusion about the relationship between the rule of law and the several claimants to nationality — whether Aboriginals, *pure laine* Quebeckers, or others — is at the heart of our recent constitutional problems. One thing at least was clear to our nineteenth-century predecessors: the European model of a nation state and a European understanding of nationalism could have no place in Canada. That was the real reason why Cartier spoke of Canada as a *political* nation.

The evidence is obvious: the French Canadians of Canada East would never agree to a nation state after struggling successfully for a hundred years to preserve their language, religion, and culture. Canada would have to bring together two very different peoples in one political structure. Brown himself explicitly rejected European precedents during the Confederation debates in the Canadian legislature in 1865: "We are endeavouring to adjust harmoniously greater difficulties than have plunged other countries into all the horrors of civil war. We are striving to do peacefully and satisfactorily what Holland and Belgium, after years of strife, were unable to accomplish. We are seeking by calm discussion to settle questions that Austria and Hungary, that Denmark and Germany, that Russia and Poland, could only crush by the iron heel of armed force." Canada has, indeed, avoided civil war, strife, and the iron heel of armed force. It is, of course, an open question whether the absence of national pride, which is practically the self-definition of a Canadian, is a consequence or a cause of our domestic tranquillity. Not that Canadians are particularly gentle, either as individuals or as armies, but that our capacity to do violence to other human beings has had minimal political significance. If the founders of Canada could not emulate the nation states of Europe, they were also unwilling to copy the United States. The Americans, they believed, had got it all wrong from the start, first by seceding from Britain and then by designing a constitution that was bound to lead to the civil war that had just ended after having cost half a million lives, more than the rest of America's wars combined. Besides, Brown and Macdonald were perfectly happy with British liberty and constitutional monarchy, so the abstract and theoretical question of improving on what was already excellent never arose.

For Brown and the other Fathers of Confederation, then, neither the European model of the national state nor the republican democracy of the United States served as useful examples for Canada to follow in trying to build and preserve a new and diverse nation. They concluded that Canada's foundation could not be built on a commonly held nationalism in a European mode, and would not be built on a great constitutional experiment. It would maintain the British connection, to be sure, but would also resemble the U.S. federation in being based on the low but solid foundations of economic self-interest. Since economic self-interest was largely responsible for bringing the Fathers of Confederation and the colonies they represented together in the first place, that was a fully intelligible turn of events. Thus was born the idea of the "new nationality" that the *Globe* had so praised on Canada's first day.

The New Nationality received its most complete expression in the speeches of George-Etienne Cartier and John A. Macdonald in the Canadian legislature in February 1865 when the Confedera-

tion scheme was being debated. One of the most vociferous opponents of Confederation, Antoine Aimé Dorion, leader of the Parti
Rouge of Canada East, had claimed that the creation of this new
nationality, so extravagantly celebrated by the supporters of Confederation, meant that French-Canadian culture would be sub-
merged. No, proclaimed Cartier, Dorion had it all wrong: "Nations
were now formed by the agglomeration of communities having
kindred interests and sympathies. Such was our case at the present
moment.... Had the diversity of race impeded the glory, the
progress, the wealth of England? ... In our own Federation we
should have Catholic and Protestant, English, French, Irish and
Scotch, and each by his efforts and his success would increase the
prosperity and glory of the new Confederacy." Cartier's political
nation would indeed gain legitimacy among all the constituent
ethnic groups, as well as among the suspicious colonial politicians,
because kindred interests and diversities of many kinds would all
benefit from the enhanced prosperity that the new nation
promised. By emphasizing what the communities and individuals
had in common rather than what divided them, Cartier's prudence
turned a potentially destructive action into a win-win achievement. All sides benefited and no one was short-changed.

In one of his contributions to the debate, Macdonald likewise
stressed the great economic powers that the Confederation agreement would confer on the new government, powers that would
enable it to achieve the prosperity and glory that Cartier spoke of:
"any honorable member on examining the list of different subjects
which are to be assigned to the general and local legislatures
respectively, will see that all the great questions which affect the
general interests of the Confederacy as a whole, are confided to
the Federal Parliament." And what were those? "The power of
dealing with the public debt and property of the Confederation ...

the regulation of trade and commerce, of customs and excise ...
the sovereign power of raising money from such sources and by
such means as the representatives of the people will allow." A
strong central government was justified by the pro-Confederates
because it would promote the general prosperity of all Canadians
and not because Macdonald favoured big government and the
trappings of monarchic splendour for federal politicians.

We make this observation not to claim that achieving economic
purposes was the exclusive aim of all the founders of Confederation. Certainly George Brown, for one, could wax eloquent about
destiny, eventual continental expansion, and construction of a
great British American nation on the northern half of the continent. So too did Cartier and Macdonald, for that matter. There was
more than just a touch of national feeling, even patriotism of a
type, expressed in the Confederation debates, in the colonial legislatures, and in the speeches and newspaper editorials of pro-Confederates. But for the most part, these men believed that doing
great things as a nation would follow from, and would be stimulated by, the establishment of an economically strong central government. Questions of language, culture, schooling, and so on,
were not important enough to warrant being placed on a list of
powers reserved for Ottawa; tariffs, taxes, the printing of money,
and the construction of railways were clearly of the first importance. Only when the national government was able to marshal
effectively the resources of the nation and to direct westward
expansion, settlement, railway construction, and industrial development would the real aim of Confederation be achieved —
namely, prosperity as a British Dominion. As long as that happened, the New Nationality would hold together out of self-interest and the mutual support of disparate groups in the common
enterprise of what we now call nation building.

The New Nationality would not receive its fullest expression unless it represented a national consensus. That consensus was to be based on four fundamentals: Ontario (and other parts of English-speaking Canada) wanted continental expansion; Quebec wanted to be secure within its own boundaries as *the* national homeland for French-speaking Canadians and to be accepted as such by English-speaking Canada; everyone wanted economic development to bring a higher standard of living; and no one was to upset this delicate arrangement, either by trying to blend French-speaking and English-speaking Canadians into a single people with what we now would call a single identity, or by trying to impose the will of the one on the other.

So, with a few exceptions, the following consensus compromise was reached: French were not to assimilate into a majority culture. English were not to attempt to undermine French culture. Scottish and Irish, Germans and Norwegians, and all the rest could continue to be Scottish, Irish, German, or whatever, provided they abided by the rules of the British parliamentary system. There was also another unspoken agreement, a kind of silent consensus compromise: no one would raise fundamental questions regarding the precise nature of the New Nationality, particularly hypothetical and abstract questions. No one, for example, raised the question of whether the French and the English were to have equal rights in the West. The assumption that lay behind this silence regarding Confederation was that English and French, Protestant and Catholic, would probably never agree on what should be taught in the schools, but they would most certainly work together to sustain national prosperity, and that was enough. In the words of Alfred Dubuc writing in "The Decline of Confederation and the New Nationalism": "Confederation was essentially an instrument of public finance whose object it was to make available to those responsible for effecting investment, the resources necessary for the unified economic development of the British colonies in North America. It was based on a fundamental project of economic growth." It could not have been based on anything else, as Cartier pointed out: "It [is] lamented by some that we had this diversity of races, and hopes [have been] expressed that this distinctive feature would cease. The idea of unity of races was utopian — it was impossible. Distinctions of this kind would always exist." So far as the economic purposes of Canada were concerned, such "distinctions" were distinctly secondary.

There would be no national myths to tie the disparate peoples of Canada together, other than the myths and ties of commerce. The role of the new national state that had been created to foster the new nationality was to promote economic growth and national development. The Fathers of Confederation well knew that the state could never have any other role. That is one reason why the federal government was given no powers over what we now call cultural matters, or over education, and why it had the preponderance of powers over commercial and economic matters. In essence, then, individual and collective self-interest was to be the glue that would hold this new nation together. It was a nation that would be "new" not only in that its legal constitution was of recent vintage, but also in that it was an experiment in creating a different kind of country. In this respect Canada was as much an experiment as the United States. For the generation of Macdonald and Cartier, it was clear from the slaughter of the War between the States that the American experiment was not an unqualified success. The weakness of the American regime, they argued, must never be duplicated in Canada. The most important flaws in the design of the American experiment were, all agreed, to be found in the relative weakness of the central government. In addition,

Americans relied perhaps too greatly on the power of their own ideas and arguments, on reason more than tradition, and on a strong faith in republican virtue. Given the ethnic and religious diversity of British North America, prudence dictated that it was perhaps wiser not to raise exciting and fundamental questions for which agreement would likely prove elusive. *Not* to raise them was, of course, a risk, for human beings everywhere are apt to want reasons for doing political things and they are not always satisfied when it is pointed out to them that it is in their interests to go along. A Burkean appeal to "prejudice" may be as risky as the American notion of appealing to self-evident truths.

Macdonald and Cartier and their allies would doubtless have dismissed such considerations as metaphysical and speculative. Their task was to demonstrate the clear benefits of union. What today we call the process of nation building began almost as soon as the new federal government began to function. As early as November of 1867 the Canadian Parliament moved to authorize the construction of the Intercolonial Railway that would link Ontario and Quebec to the Maritime provinces, and began the manoeuvring by which Canada would soon obtain Rupert's Land and thereby acquire the territory of the present prairie provinces and much of the North. That task was completed in 1868 and 1869. Rupert's Land became Manitoba and the North-West Territories in 1870, after the Red River Rebellion led by Louis Riel had been dealt with.

Urged on by London, in 1870, Canada and British Columbia began negotiations to join the two possessions of the Crown. One of the terms eventually settled upon (British Columbia entered Confederation in 1871) was the construction of a railway to the Pacific coast. In 1872 Parliament passed the Dominion Lands Act, which provided for a massive survey of the potential agricultural land of the prairies and its division into homesteads. It also established the conditions by which settlers could acquire title to western farms. These involved paying a small registration fee ($10), living on the homestead, and developing it or "proving it up" over a three-year period by putting in crops and establishing permanent buildings. At the same time, the task of enticing the Indians of the West was begun. Treaty No. 1 was concluded in July 1871 and Treaty No. 7, the last of the general "numbered" treaties with the plains Indians of the southern prairies, was signed six years later. These were essentially what we would now call land-claim settlements, not treaties in the European sense of agreements between sovereign powers. The consequence was that Indians were settled on lands reserved exclusively for them and the remaining territory was "thrown open," in the language of the day, to agricultural settlement.

Thus, by 1872 Macdonald's government had extended the boundaries of Canada to the Pacific, established the laws by which the West was to be settled and initiated the survey of the West, started moving the Indians onto reserved land, and begun the Pacific railway. But in Macdonald's mind the most important step the national government could take was to establish a tariff policy that would protect Canadian manufacturing. As his biographer, Donald Creighton, observed: "the impulse towards economic nationalism was potent ... with a sure instinct for the telling slogan [Macdonald] appropriated a phrase, 'National Policy,' which others had used incidentally, but never so purposefully before." The National Policy was originally a policy of high protective tariffs and nothing else; eventually, Macdonald and the Conservative party packaged it together with construction of the CPR and western settlement, and sold it to the voters as a cohesive approach to national development. Industry would provide the goods, the railway would carry both the goods and the settlers, the settlers would consume the goods — as would the factory hands who would make them. It was a neat package, easy to sell (harder to do, of course), that would appear to embody the reasons why the British American colonists had come together in the first place.

It would take decades before the National Policy would produce tangible results, not all of them anticipated even by the cautious Macdonald. The Pacific railway was delayed. The Pacific Scandal forced Macdonald from office as a result of shady deals made by him with American railway promoters and Montreal shipping magnate Sir Hugh Allan. That scandal tainted the Pacific railway project in the eyes of the Liberal government that succeeded Macdonald. But even if it had not, Canada, along with much of the industrialized world of that day, was plunged into recession. There was no government money to build the railway and no entrepreneurs willing to take it on. It was not until 1880 that a re-elected Macdonald government could entice a respectable syndicate with a most lucrative contract. The Canadian Pacific Railway was completed in 1885.

From the point of view of western settlement, it was just as well. Surveying the West was a huge job. It went slowly. The settlers stayed away in legions, preferring the more hospitable United States. Although some immigrants did come from Europe (mostly Britain), the United States, and Ontario, the population of the prairies was barely 120,000 at the time of the 1881 census. It was not until the late 1890s, and the closing of the frontier in the United States, that the real flood tide of immigrants began.

Initially, Canadian tariff policy was not very successful either. Following Macdonald's return to office in 1878, hefty tariff increases were introduced on a wide range of products, but the country was still mired in recession. It was not until the late 1880s that Canada truly began to develop a substantial manufacturing sector, mostly in central Canada.

The articulation of the National Policy marked one of the most successful feats of political salesmanship in Canadian history. All attempts by the opposition Liberals throughout the 1880s and early 1890s to provide an alternative failed. In 1891, for example, the Liberals ran on a policy of freer trade with the United States; Macdonald fought what proved to be his last campaign on the platform of "The Old Flag [the Union Jack], the Old Policy, and the Old Leader" and whipped the Grits. The Liberals, led by Wilfrid Laurier, then saw the light; prior to the next federal election in 1896 they assured the business community and the voters that they would not trifle with the National Policy. In fact, it was under Laurier's Liberal government that the National Policy saw its greatest successes.

Why was the National Policy so successful, even though it did not always work smoothly — and undeniably forced up the living costs of Canadians? One answer, given by historian Craig Brown in his article "The Nationalism of the National Policy," was that the National Policy embodied the very reasons why colonists had become Canadians in the first place: "Macdonald was looking for a policy that would attract, at one and the same time, voters and dollars to his party, and the National Policy would do both. The manufacturers would contribute to the party war-chest and the simplicity of the title and concept of the National Policy would appeal to an electorate looking to fulfill the promise of Confederation." This was the age of expansion, when the United States was flinging a nation across the continent, building continent-spanning railways, putting the Great Plains to the plough, and claiming an empire on the Pacific coast. Canada would do the same, and Canadians "could take pride in their ability to compete with their neighbours in the conquest of the continent."

But there was more to the attractiveness of the National Policy than this. The solid but dull foundation of prosperity would be tied to the exciting prospects of nation building and the respectable and inspirational myth of progress. In practice, several things were implied. First of all, the National Policy was to be the means by which Canadians would cease to be simple "hewers of wood and drawers of water" for the United States; Canadians would, instead, seize their own economic destiny and shape their future through their own industrial development. It was, quite simply, the means by which they would turn the evocation of a new nationality into a reality. The National Policy promised to give a real and tangible meaning to being Canadian. It held out the promise of success based on common purposes, common tasks, and a better future. Canadian nationalism would come into being at the same time as future achievements provided evidence that the project was worth the effort. Unlike citizens of European nations, it was impossible for Canadians to look back upon centuries of labour or upon glorious military deeds. They looked ahead, and confidently expected their own creativity to be sufficient to actualize the new political nation.

Besides the National Policy and confidence in the future, there was another, less visible, reason why Macdonald's party dominated Canadian politics in the three decades after Confederation: patronage. Macdonald had not invented patronage, of course, but he elevated it to a high art in Canadian politics. His Tory party was held together by an intricate network of judgeships, postmasterships, appointments to commissions, and so on. Even militia officers were primarily patronage appointments. Nor did Macdonald leave the business of patronage to underlings. It was his business as party leader and prime minister to oversee the filling of government posts, major and minor. Patronage was used not only to reward friends, but to cement loyalties and to fight those within his own party whom he considered dangerous to the party and to his understanding of the nation's interests. Here too was a raw self-interest that anyone could understand and that every party leader and office holder could appreciate. The Liberal premier of Ontario, Oliver Mowat, used patronage as assiduously as Macdonald and for the same reasons. So did Wilfrid Laurier, for that matter. Thus patronage was a useful and effective instrument that helped forge the national consensus and keep the attention of politically minded Canadians focused on economic self-interest.

By the mid-1880s, then, Canada's original purposes seemed nearly to be fulfilled. Confederation had brought a disparate group of colonists together in a political union that was essentially anti-nationalist in the European sense, in that it eschewed the familiar forms and trappings of nineteenth-century nationalism. Canada looked to the future, not to the past. Canada was not built on a commonality of history, language, religion, culture, or ethnicity. Nor was it built on a widespread acceptance of fundamental rational and self-evident ideas about the relationship people ought to have to their governments, as the United States had been. It was founded on the belief that economic self-interest was the strongest glue of all; the National Policy was seized upon by many Canadians as the means by which that economic self-interest would achieve fruition, and patronage was both the carrot and the stick by which Macdonald kept most of the government's supporters in check and marching to the same tune.

As time wore on and the West gained in population, in self-confidence, and in political maturity, the effects of the National Policy seemed less beneficial, at least to westerners. Even so, the westerners' criticisms were (and remain) essentially economic ones. But all policies, especially successful ones that actually change political or economic conditions, lead to unintended and unanticipated results. However the results of the National Policy are judged (and we believe that reasonable people may disagree about it), the intended direction was fundamentally sound: economic prosperity and individual liberty were the twin and complementary bases, not a collectivist evocation of the public good or some abstract notion of public virtue, not religious truth or cultural integrity, and nothing so empty as communal self-development.

In terms of the distinction made in chapter 1 between liberal and communitarian approaches to government, it is clear that the Fathers of Confederation were among the liberals. And yet there were always some Canadians who believed that economic self-interest was not enough and who yearned to build a nation based on those mystical collectivist bonds of culture, history, and language that seemed to them to form the bases of European nationhood. For them, politics had to be something more than just a question of whether or not railway ties, or coal, or cotton cloth, were to be taxed at this *ad valorem* rate or that. Politics had to have a vertical, though hardly a transcendent, dimension to it as well as a mundane one. For these communitarians, politics included a search for higher meaning, for more fundamental values, for greater public virtue. Otherwise, they said, it was nothing more than an expression of base interest and a vehicle for corrupt practices.

The earliest Canadian manifestation of such a view was the Canada First movement, founded in 1868. This small group of largely Ontario men set for themselves the task of providing a cultural and intellectual soul for the economic creature that Macdonald and the other Fathers of Confederation had created. Since there was little obvious common ground between French, Catholic

Quebec and English, Protestant Ontario, their task was daunting, to say the least. It amounted to nothing less than an attempt to invent a common definition of "Canadianism" that a majority of their fellow Canadians might accept and that was not based on what they considered to be the superficial and even corrupt ties of economic self-interest. Their motives were pure, but their destiny was failure. Even so, they are worth examining because they provide the foil for the practical-minded men who actually put the country together and saw that it worked. Also, they are the intellectual predecessors of the Conservative and Liberal governments that attempted to do the very same thing a century later, and with equally dismal results.

Canada First was founded by George Denison, Henry Morgan, Charles Mair, and William Foster from Ontario, and Robert G. Haliburton, a Nova Scotian living in Ottawa. In the words of *The Canadian Encyclopedia*, Canada First "sought to promote a sense of national purpose and lay the intellectual foundations for Canadian nationality." Such promotional activity was difficult to do in a country as obviously divided along linguistic and religious lines as Canada. Nevertheless, these men searched for defining characteristics that both French-speaking and English-speaking Canadians might be said to have in common. It was obviously not language. Nor was it religion or culture. Something hidden but more fundamental had to be found or invented. And so they argued that since most Quebeckers traced their roots to Normandy, and since Britain had been conquered by the Normans under William the Conqueror in 1066, it followed (at least to the Canada Firsters) that there were common historical and, more important, "racial" ties binding French and English together. The appeal to events 800 years earlier in Europe as providing meaningful guidance to contemporary affairs among Canadian backwoodsmen indicates a great power of abstraction and a great absence of common sense. In this respect at least they were fully the equal of their twentieth-century counterparts.

Canada First also tried to unite English-speaking and French-speaking Canadians by emphasizing large and remote political objectives upon which both groups might agree, such as independence from Britain. They betrayed a basic ignorance of Quebec in this, because Quebeckers were not interested in a Canadian independence that might leave them to the tender mercies of the English-speaking majority. French Quebec was loyal to the British Crown for the perfectly obvious reason that the British Crown guaranteed Quebeckers protection at a time when they had neither the skill nor the will to protect themselves. It was, however, less the Canada Firsters' pretensions in creating an independent foreign policy than their efforts to create a Canadian nationalism based on a Darwinian notion of environmental determinism that is most revealing.

One of the earliest attempts came from the pen of Robert Grant Haliburton. In 1869 he gave an address to the Montreal Literary Club entitled "We are the Northmen of the New World." The most important defining characteristic of Canada was, he asserted, that it "must ever be that it is a Northern country inhabited by the descendants of Northern races." W.A. Foster echoed that idea: "The old Norse Mythology, with its Thor hammers and Thor hammering, appeals to us, — for we are a Northern people, — as the true out-crop of human nature, more manly, more real, than the weak marrow-bones superstition of an effeminate South." It was this "northernness" that not only united Canadians, but gave them their strong adherence to self-government and their self-reliance. It also gave them a common history, Canada First believed, no matter which side of the battle line they had been on in the Battle of the Plains of Abraham.

Canada First was never more than a small handful of intellectuals; it had some larger impact on the Canadian political scene during the Red River Rebellion in the North-West in 1869–70, when it championed the cause of the small expatriate Ontario community at Red River. After Riel's provisional government executed Thomas Scott, a young Ontario Orangeman who had been caught after an attempted escape from Riel's custody, the members of Canada First helped elevate Scott into a martyr for the cause of Canadian expansionism. For the most part, however, the movement had little immediate impact beyond its fostering of the northern myth, which is with us still in the words of the English-language version of the Canadian national anthem. Fortunately, the true north strong and free rid itself of all the Thor hammers and Thor hammering.

Canada First could not succeed. In retrospect, its creators appear to be little more than a few fevered intellectuals yearning for an existing collective meaning because they were unable to find satisfaction in their individual lives. The intellectual ideas of the movement never caught the public's imagination. The public, it seemed, had more practical as well as better things to do. For all their proclamations that they were simply Canadians first, their appeal was lost on French-speaking Canadians, who could hardly be expected to abandon the British connection when they contemplated the fate of Louis Riel. Macdonald and the other members of the political élite who forged the Confederation agreements were too powerful, too sensible, and too pervasive; there was never any chance that Macdonald's primacy in the halls of power could be challenged by a group of poetic dreamers. Canada First actually entered politics as the Canadian National Association in 1874; its journal, the *Nation*, enjoyed some success, and Liberal leader Edward Blake flirted with Canada First for a time. But in the end its appeal was too limited for success even in Ontario, and its increasingly anti-Catholic tone condemned it to complete failure in Quebec.

But Canada First could never have succeeded no matter what tactics it adopted; its efforts to find common cultural or national grounds upon which Canadians could build a true national sentiment foundered on the hard rocks of reality; there were no such grounds; there truly were fundamental differences of language, religion, culture, and historical experience separating Canadians. It was easy to declare in stentorian tones that both French-speaking and English-speaking Canadians had fought to push back the forest and "tame" or subdue the "savages," but the French certainly knew that what they had done most of the time was fight the English and resist the conquest that eventually befell them. Evidently it *did* matter which side of the battle one identified with at the Plains of Abraham, and no amount of inventive evocation of William the Conqueror or the hammerings of Thor would change that.

So Macdonald and economic pragmatism won the day in a battle that was always far from equal. And, it must be said, Macdonald's Liberal opponents saw the new nation little differently than he did. The Liberal interregnum between 1874 and 1878 that resulted from Macdonald's disgrace in the Pacific Scandal, saw no change in Macdonaldian pragmatism. The Liberals governed during the depths of a recession and so could not prosecute schemes as grand as those of Macdonald, but they pushed ahead with the practical needs of nation building just the same. From 1874 to 1878 most of the survey work necessary to the completion of the Pacific railway went ahead, as did a modest amount of construction (financed as a public work) while the signing of agreements with the Indians, the establishment of the North-West Mounted Police, and the survey of Dominion lands into homesteads also continued. The Liberals did not raise tariffs, but they didn't drop them either. They also introduced a number of political reforms, such as the secret ballot. What they did not do was also important. Most significantly, they did not stimulate debate over the fundamental nature of Canada. They believed, as Macdonald did, that their role was to provide good government through national development and economic stability; it was not to help Canadians find their illusive collective soul or national identity; nor was it to promote public virtue.

Wilfrid Laurier continued to pursue the goal of good government. After the execution of Louis Riel in November 1885 for treason (he had led the North-West Rebellion earlier that year), some Quebeckers urged the establishment of a Parti National as a reaction to the execution. Their aim was to unite Quebeckers in one party, thus increasing what was later called "French power" in Canada. Laurier was strongly opposed to such a move. He knew well that parties based upon religion or language would help destroy the implicit consensus upon which Confederation was based: "It would be simply suicidal to French Canadians to form a party by themselves. Why, so soon as French Canadians, who are in a minority in this House and in the country, were to organize as a political party, they would compel the [English-speaking] majority to organize as a political party, and the result must be disastrous to themselves.... *This country must be governed and can be governed simply on questions of policy and administration.*" Laurier's "policy and administration" is the very definition of good government. He knew as well as Macdonald that bread-and-butter issues, not ideas, were the pith and substance of Canadian politics. Like Keats, they knew that the mighty abstract idea stifles domestic happiness, and they knew as well where political priorities lay.

It is clear that from Confederation to the end of the nineteenth century (and, as we will see, in most of the first half of the twentieth), Canada's prime ministers and the governments they led — Macdonald, Mackenzie, Laurier — knew that their mandate was to steer clear of the thorny grounds of religion and culture, of what we now call questions of Canadian identity, and use the substantial economic powers that Ottawa had under the BNA Act to organize and guide national economic development. They eschewed the search for political virtue or fundamental values that had been the sole *raison d'être* of those who had, for example, founded the Canada First movement. Starting in the 1880s, however, the challenges to that prudent course grew with each passing year, put forward by men and women whose views on Canada's destiny were very different from those of Canada First but who shared one fundamental principle — that politics was nothing if not a search for higher purposes and that it was the duty of the state to lead the quest for public virtue. Pragmatic success, it seems, inspires discontent in visionaries, who always want something more. Instead of looking for it in a life of contemplation or religious devotion or even in the happiness of family domesticity, they insist on a "cause" and are bound and determined to use the political stage to promote it. In Canadian experience, and elsewhere too, all such efforts lead to what Burke called "settled mismanagement."

The initial challenge to the economic fundamentalism of Macdonald, Mackenzie, and Laurier came from English-speaking Canada, not from Quebec. It came primarily from those who saw no future in Canada-as-it-was, and who wanted their country to become an integral part of an expanding British Empire that had become globe-spanning in its power and its proportions. That sentiment was well expressed by yet another intellectual, the Reverend Dr. King, principal of Manitoba College, in 1889: "We must either have a different and a closer connection with the Empire, or, we shall be inevitably absorbed by the great nation to the South…. Independence in the case of a people situated as we are, is not to be thought of…. Five millions of Canadians are not going to remain for an indefinite time, or indeed for a much longer time, subjects of an Empire in the highest issues of which they have no voice." Rev. King and others (the most prominent was Principal George Grant of Queen's University) pushed for a great federation that would unite Britain with Canada and the other self-governing (that is, white) colonies of the Empire. The attractions of imperial power were obvious to them, and they responded by founding Canadian chapters of the Imperial Federation League, first established in the United Kingdom in 1884. But there were other manifestations of a growing search for "identity" in English-speaking Canada that threatened the Confederation consensus even more. Much of the Ontario chauvinism that accompanied the mounting of the military expedition to put down Riel's North-West Rebellion was couched in imperialist rhetoric about Canada's manifest destiny and the need to put the Métis, especially the French Métis, in their proper place. The most violent of the rhetoric came after Riel was sentenced to death during the national debate as to whether or not the government should carry out the sentence. Some of the Tory press in Ontario went so far as to accuse all French-speaking Canadians of harbouring traitorous sentiments. Here, truly, were men with a cause.

The uproar over the North-West Rebellion and the hanging of Riel, combined with the rising rhetoric of English-speaking imperialist chauvinism, laid the groundwork for D'Alton McCarthy. Born in 1836 near Dublin, McCarthy came to Canada as a boy. A dedicated Tory, he was first elected to Parliament representing the riding of North Simcoe in 1876. In 1889 he broke with his party to launch the Equal Rights Association (ERA), which had, as its slogan, "equal rights for all, special privileges for none." On the surface, McCarthy's slogan looks liberal enough, a mere repetition of the doctrine of equal protection by the laws. But in context it had, and was intended to have, an entirely different meaning. It was not intended as a reminder of what already existed; it was not a repetition of a familiar legal precept at all, but an aggressive initiative.

The evidence is clear enough. McCarthy broke with the Tories allegedly over the resolution, by the Quebec government, of the Jesuit Estates question in 1888. That question stemmed from the confiscation by the British of Jesuit property following New France's transfer to the sovereign jurisdiction of Britain in 1763. The settlement, concluded with the aid of Pope Leo XIII, saw the Quebec government allot some $400,000 to the Jesuits, to Laval University, and to other Catholic orders and $60,000 to Quebec's Protestant schools. The matter was solely within Quebec's jurisdiction as defined by the BNA Act. It was, however, challenged by extremist Protestant groups in Ontario on the grounds of papal interference. It was Protestants in Ontario, not Catholics in Quebec, who first injected religion into the political discourse of the nation. And with religion came all the ancillary things that prudent men had sought to exclude from political life: language, culture, and the million trivialities that divide individuals one from another. It was an act of remarkable stupidity. In the aftermath of the ensuing uproar, McCarthy founded the ERA.

The ERA was determined to expunge the French language from the West (even McCarthy saw it was a fool's mission to try the same thing in Quebec) and to destroy the system of tax-supported separate (i.e., Catholic) schools that had existed in Manitoba since 1870 and the North-West since 1875. It might well have aimed also at separate schools in Ontario, but they were guaranteed by the BNA Act and, therefore, not likely to be vulnerable. The lobbying of the ERA was one factor behind the decision of the Manitoba government to end tax support for Catholic schools in 1890, a move that precipitated the Manitoba Schools Question. There is no need to provide a blow-by-blow account of the struggle for separate schools in Manitoba except to say that the political crisis lasted for much of the decade. We would, however, point out that McCarthy and his followers were trying to move Canada a long way from the economic fundamentalism of Macdonald and the Fathers of Confederation. Macdonald knew it; and he fought McCarthy not because he had an ingrained sympathy for French and Catholic rights in the West, but because McCarthy represented a threat to the Tory party and the implicit national consensus to which that party was dedicated. Laurier fought McCarthy as well and charged him with "opening the flood-gates to passions which, once aroused, perhaps no human power may be able to restrain. He is appealing to national and religious passions, the most inflexible of all passions." Laurier might have added that had Macdonald or Brown or Cartier done the same in 1864, there would have been no Canada.

The passions aroused by the Riel uprising, the Equal Rights Association, English-Canadian imperialism, and the Manitoba Schools Question made it increasingly difficult for federal leaders to walk the straight and narrow path of economic fundamentalism. Sometimes they didn't. When Catholic parents fought the Manitoba government in the courts, they lost their case but were told that they could approach Ottawa to seek repeal of the provincial legislation under section 93 of the BNA Act. They did, and Tory prime minister Sir Charles Tupper (Macdonald had died in 1891) responded with a federal bill to restore separate schools in that province. But Laurier, though French and Catholic, opposed Tupper, led a Liberal filibuster in the House, and delayed passage of the measure until the government's mandate ran out. In the election that followed (June 23, 1896) he vowed that he would not interfere in provincial matters and would, instead, use "sunny ways," that is, negotiation and conciliation, to seek redress for Catholic parents in Manitoba. After he was elected, he did just that and was able to win some small concessions from the Manitoba government, but not the restoration of tax support for Catholic schools.

Laurier's refusal to intervene directly in Manitoba's educational affairs was partly a consequence of political expediency, partly of his belief in provincial rights. But it was also an illustration of his view that it was not the business of the federal government to impose a predetermined concept of "Canada" either on the provinces or on the people. Laurier has often been charged with doing an about-face some years later when Ottawa established Alberta and Saskatchewan with tax-supported separate schools. But in fact the Autonomy Bills of 1905 actually extended a school system that had been in effect since 1875; there was nothing new about separate schools in the new provinces of Alberta and Saskatchewan. In effect, Laurier's approach was to steer clear of federal intervention in religious or cultural affairs and concentrate, instead, on economic development. In this he was following directly in Macdonald's trail of economic fundamentalism and good government.

Much of Laurier's effort at economic development was unsuccessful. Where there was one transcontinental railway when he came to power, there were three when he left, and two were virtually bankrupt. The government, directly and through favoured companies, ran up a massive railway debt that Canada continued to pay for decades after. Much of Laurier's motive was pure politics

— to enhance the fortunes of the Liberal party the way the CPR had shored up the Tories. Nevertheless, it is not his purity of motive or acuity as a developer that is at issue here. The fact is that he continued the Macdonaldian vision of keeping away from danger, eschewing cultural politics, and concentrating his energies on economic development, which is what the country was put together for in the first place.

He had a less easy time when it came to handling the rising tide of imperialist sentiment in English-speaking Canada, especially after the outbreak of the Boer War in South Africa in 1899. There can be little real doubt that if he had been free to choose between closer ties with the Empire or gradual but discernible evolution to full national autonomy, Laurier would have chosen the latter. He was well aware that French Canada would never accept the former because it was so closely tied to British doctrines of ethnic supremacy. Indeed, closer imperial cooperation automatically raised symbolic questions about language, religion, and culture that were by definition dangerous to the Canadian consensus. As Henri Bourassa pointed out on several occasions, a national consensus could not be built as long as French-speaking Canadians owed allegiance only to Canada while many English-speaking Canadians could not make up their minds whether to love Canada or the British Empire. What Bourassa did not understand, or accept, was that many English-speaking Canadians of British origin thought of Canada as little more than an outlying region of the Empire and saw no dichotomy. This is why so many Canadian politicians of the day spoke fondly of "home" and meant the British Isles. They did so in spite of the fact that in many instances they had not laid eyes upon "this scepter'd isle ... this precious stone set in the silver sea," since childhood. Some had even been born on this side of the Atlantic.

On the two great imperial questions that Laurier faced as prime minister, namely whether Canada should participate in the Boer War and whether (and on what terms) Canada should contribute to the overall defence of the British Empire, he tried to steer a middle way. Canadians fought in South Africa, but not as an official Canadian contingent; Canada would build its own navy but would not contribute directly to Britain's defence budget. But with the national consensus breaking down in the streets and in the editorial offices and pulpits of the nation, Laurier's middle way was uncertain indeed and left many French-speaking and English-speaking Canadians dissatisfied. Laurier had the misfortune to govern at a time when those who sought to tie Canada more closely to the Empire, the Imperial Federationists, and those who wanted to promote Canadian independence, Bourassa and his followers, were determined to inject their own brand of public virtue into national politics. Laurier's defeat in 1911 on a proposal to cement a reciprocity agreement with the United States — a measure that all Canadian governments, whether Liberal or Tory, had sought since before Confederation — was largely a result of that search for public virtue. It mattered not a whit that the Imperial Federationists and Bourassa disagreed more with one another than they did with Laurier: moderation, pragmatism, and prudence were coming under attack by men with visions and a cause.

Laurier's Conservative successor, Robert Borden, would have tried to steer the nation's attention back to economic fundamentalism if he could have. Despite his reputation for being unsympathetic to French Canada, earned largely as a result of the conscription crisis of 1917, Borden was well aware from the start of how destructive religious, cultural, and language questions could be. Although many Quebeckers opposed his intention to contribute directly to the British naval construction program rather than create a Canadian navy, the measure was not in itself anti-Quebec.

But contribution to the Royal Navy was something forced upon him by outside events; his original domestic agenda was, in the language of the day, progressive: clean up corruption in government, broaden the range of government services, rationalize the national transportation system. The outbreak of war in August 1914 forced him to put that agenda to the side.

Borden's response to the war was essentially pragmatic; there is no evidence that he intended to use the war to steer Canada in some predetermined direction, or that he wanted to design a Canada according to some artificial sense of "destiny." It is quite true that Borden gave Canada a major push on the road to full autonomy with his insistence in 1917 that Canada and the other self-governing dominions should be treated as full partners in the war effort. But this arose not out of any theoretical or abstract consideration; it came from the practical reality that the government and people of Canada were making a major contribution to the Allied war effort with four heavy infantry divisions on the western front. Borden simply insisted on having a say on how those troops were going to be used. Similarly, his single-minded pursuit of conscription, over the intense opposition of Quebec, was rooted not in any desire to force Quebeckers into an imperial mould, but in his belief that Canada's credibility as a nation depended on its keeping faith with the troops, all volunteers, who were already there. If the Canadian contingent at the front were to be allowed to shrink to insignificance through attrition, then the sacrifices that Canada's soldiers had already made would surely have been in vain. Borden's point, after all, was that this had become a Canadian war as well as a British and French one. For that reason, if for no other, Canada had a duty to see it through.

Borden's pragmatism was not appreciated by those in Quebec who saw conscription as the ultimate symbolic horror — forcing them to risk life and limb in the trenches of the western front for the same British Empire that had made of them a conquered people. Of course, it was not for the British Empire that this sacrifice was being asked as much as it was for Canada-as-it-was. And even if it *was* for the Empire, it was the same Empire to which both Laurier and Bourassa had many times sworn allegiance, the same Empire that had extended political liberty to a religious and cultural minority it once had conquered on the field of battle. But no matter; the damage was done. Symbolic politics overwhelmed Borden's pragmatism and Canada was torn apart. Those very passions of language and religion that Laurier had warned against in attacking McCarthy, passions that, had they been unleashed in the early 1860s would have made Canada impossible, were unleashed in the 1917 election, one of the sorriest spectacles that Canadian politics has yet seen. Whatever Borden's original motive, the government's pitch for votes was cast in the language of political virtue; a vote for Laurier's anti-conscription Liberals was claimed by them to be a vote for the Kaiser himself.

William Lyon Mackenzie King came to office in December 1921 determined to steer the national government back to the course of economic fundamentalism and dampen the passions kindled during the war. By and large, he succeeded. That very success was scorned by at least two generations of intellectuals whose chief indictment of King was, in the words of socialist poet F.R. Scott, that

> He blunted us.
> We had no shape
> Because he never took sides,
> And no sides
> Because he never allowed them to take shape.

But this was not a result so much of any character flaw as it was of King's acute sensitivity to the reality that any federal government that was determined to mould a Canadian character was also a federal government that endangered the implicit Canadian consensus and thus the existence of Canada itself. King's view of the government's mandate was simple; provide good administration, quell passion, balance budgets wherever possible, steer clear of grandiose schemes, act from consensus to preserve consensus. It was dull, it was boring, it irritated intellectuals such as Scott who demanded ideas, ideology, a vision, passion, and a cause in their politics, and who were engaged in an endless quest for political virtue. But King's way worked. Even when his Liberal government began to move towards the welfare state in 1943, King and his ministers and chief bureaucrats couched their effort in the language of economic efficiency. They were not so much building a fantasy land of "social justice" as they were providing for full employment, a goal that even Macdonald would have approved.

In fact, social welfare and unemployment insurance under King had a distinctly utilitarian tone. They were to serve Canadians in social or economic need the way police or fire departments do; they were there when needed and were funded at public expense, but they were there *only* when needed and not to be counted upon at all times by all Canadians as a matter of right. That was a basic difference in philosophy from the attitudes of most of King's successors.

In the first eight decades of Confederation, then, prime ministers and their governments steered clear of any effort to tell Canadians who and what they were, or ought to be. The role of the Canadian state was just as it had been laid out in the residual clause of the BNA Act — "peace, order, and good government." Those like the Canada Firsters, or the Imperial Federationists, or the Equal Rights Association, or Bourassa's Ligue Canadien Nationaliste, or indeed Frank Scott's League for Social Reconstruction, had to be isolated and resisted; they represented the antithesis of the economic fundamentalism, the New Nationalism, that underlay the very establishment of the country. Leaders from Macdonald to King knew that it was simply not possible to attempt to define Canada and that to make the attempt would open up abstract issues and raise symbolic questions that could never be resolved. They were liberals not collectivists. They had sufficient good sense — sufficient prudence — to know that collectivist aspirations to public virtue, however appealing they may be in an abstract intellectual sense, were no more than intellectual abstractions. They shrewdly suspected as well that those who advocated lofty visions of the public good, of national identity, of true Canadianism, were little more than abstracted intellectuals themselves. And they would have agreed with Burke that the loudest complainers for the public good were seldom the most anxious for its welfare. The opposite was more likely to be true. Quite properly, then, the politicians who governed Canada until 1945 kept to the low road: the role of the state in the great scheme of things was small. Individuals alone were capable of pursuing a life of virtue or, indeed, of forging an identity. Culture, like religion in earlier centuries, was best left in the private sphere, the sphere of civil society, as we would say today. But then, at the end of World War Two, the world, and Canada, began to change.

3
Bad Government Begins

On June 10, 1957, almost ninety years after Confederation, John George Diefenbaker was elected Prime Minister of Canada, heading a minority government. Less than one year later, on March 31, 1958, Diefenbaker won the largest majority in Canadian history up to that time, taking 208 of 265 Commons seats; the Liberals captured 49 seats, the Co-operative Commonwealth Federation (CCF) 8. Although change in the art and mechanics of governance is usually evolutionary in a democracy, Diefenbaker's government marked a watershed in Canadian history. For the first time since Confederation, Canada had a prime minister whose chief objective was social justice and whose major aim was to mould a Canadian national character in his own image. Even though Dief the Chief made a career of studying John A. Macdonald — "the Old Chieftain" — and often seemed to claim Sir John's mantle, the Chief and the Old Chieftain did very different things with the power that the electors handed them. Whereas Macdonald knew that a pursuit of public virtue had no place in Canadian national governance, Diefenbaker was determined to establish public virtue at the pinnacle of his government's objectives. Diefenbaker's real ancestors were not the prudent and pragmatic Fathers of Confederation, but the idealistic dreamers who had founded the Canada First movement.

The stage for Diefenbaker's ascension was set twelve years before, in the spring of 1945, when the bells of victory pealed across Europe. Canada played a significant part in the Allied victory in World War Two; well over a million Canadians had served in the armed forces, and the vast bulk of Canada's productive capacity was eventually directed towards the war effort. By the end of the war Canadian factories were building a wide variety of war goods, from heavy bombers to radars. Displaying its customary caution with respect to fundamental things, the King government hesitated for some time before making a major commitment to the war effort. In the event, the government borrowed heavily and ran up huge deficits relative to gross national product. In 1944, for example, the government spent a total of $5.87 billion but took in only $3.3 billion for a deficit of some $2.6 billion. That is, nearly a quarter of the government expenditures were not met by current revenue, which at the time was a huge amount.

Despite Canada's heavy indebtedness, the future looked bright in the spring of 1945. The vast bulk of the Canadian debt was held by Canadians in the form of Victory Bonds and other wartime savings schemes. In addition, it was relatively easy for the government to make massive chops in expenditures as soon as the war ended because all it had to do was slash the size of, and the expenditure on, the military. The armed forces were reduced from just over 700,000 in May 1945 to less than 30,000 by mid-1947. The federal deficit dropped to $121 million in 1946 and disappeared altogether the following year as the government began to string together successive surpluses.

There was tremendous pent-up demand within the Canadian economy in the spring of 1945. Wages and prices had been virtually frozen for years. And there had been few consumer goods to buy, even for those people with money. Canada had not seen a new car built since 1940; everything from canned fruit cocktail to gasoline had been rationed. When the million veterans returned home with their forced savings waiting for them, and aided by a comprehensive veterans' benefits program, they married, had children (the first wave of the Baby Boom) and went on a spending spree: houses, appliances, cars, clothes — all types of consumer goods had to be replaced. Canada's gross national product increased 36 per cent between 1945 ($11.81 billion) and 1949 ($16.07 billion). Despite tax reductions after the war (in the form of the removal of a variety of war taxes), the federal government's revenue from taxes increased some 26 per cent between 1945 and 1949.

In part, Canada's financial house was in such tidy shape in these postwar years because of the prudent fiscal management of the national government. Starting in 1943, the Liberal government of William Lyon Mackenzie King had started to shift to the left and had initiated plans for social welfare measures to bolster the postwar economy. Among those eventually enshrined in law were the veterans' benefits program, family allowances, price supports for certain agricultural goods, and a national housing program to be administered by a new Central Mortgage and Housing Corporation. The government had a number of aims: to guard against postwar recession; to ensure postwar social peace; to strengthen capitalism by using Keynesian economic policy to attain full employment; and, not least, to increase its chances for re-election. It was certainly successful in gaining the last objective, and won a majority in June, 1945.

The government's plans for the postwar economy were summarized in two documents, one small the other massive. The smaller one was the White Paper on Employment and Incomes, released before the 1945 election, which committed Canada to deficit financing when necessary to ensure full employment. It marked the first triumph of Keynesian thinking in Ottawa. The larger document was the Green Book of federal proposals prepared for the 1945–46 Dominion-Provincial Conference on Economic Reconstruction. It contained plans for a national health insurance scheme (among other proposals), and an extensive reworking of federal-provincial financial relations. It was, in part, an attempt to implement the recommendations of the 1937 Rowell-Sirois Commission, which had looked at Canada in the Great Depression and recommended ways to allow concerted action to be taken to combat unemployment and poverty. The conference was a failure and the Green Book proposals fell by the wayside.

Can it be said that in implementing family allowances and other social welfare measures, in introducing the White Paper on Employment and Incomes, and in formulating the Green Book proposals, the King government had substantially departed from the pre-Keynesian economic fundamentalism that had marked most Canadian national regimes up to that point? Was King trying to remake Canada in his own image? Were he and his ministers pursuing public virtue?

Much of the political rhetoric of the 1945 election would have given that impression. But an examination of the reality behind the rhetoric shows that the government was actually trying to do something else. It was attempting to broaden the participation of

Canadians in their own economy, to add depth to the consumer side of that economy, and to increase the number of people with a stake in the status quo. Virtually everything the King government did, from making it easier for workers to unionize and win higher wages to initiating family allowances (which were designed not as a "welfare" measure but to increase national purchasing power through a transfer of wealth from some taxpayers to all mothers), was aimed in that direction. There is no evidence that the impetus behind the government's moderate shift to the left was intended to achieve anything like what later was called social justice. As Peter Newman put it some years later: "King's social welfare measures were designed to fill demonstrated needs." There was no hint that King and his ministers were trying to mould the Canadian national character, or that they were creating a welfare state in response to some innate Canadian characteristic — such as living in a "peaceable kingdom" — that distinguished Canadians from, say, Americans. In fact, in 1945 the United States was still far ahead of Canada in the variety of welfare measures that the average American citizen could call on.

What King and company were doing was the ultimate in pragmatism. Instead of building more railways to create jobs (actually, they *did* use public works on occasion to battle seasonal and regional unemployment), they were using wealth distribution to create consumption that would create jobs. But all this was to be done in a strictly pay-as-you-go fashion that carried over into the St. Laurent era. When, for example, the federal government began to increase the defence budget dramatically in response to a rise in Cold War tensions, especially after the outbreak of the Korean War in June 1950, taxes were increased and extensions of existing welfare measures were deferred to keep the budget in line. And when the government ran surpluses, as in 1957, it took some of the surplus cash and raised old age pension benefits.

It was simply not in King's character to do anything else; he was not going to tell Canadians what being Canadian meant and he was not going to use the power of the central government to impose new theories of government or national development on other Canadians. He was not going to redistribute wealth because some compassionate theorist thought it was a bright idea. Some of his ministers were prepared to force the provinces to go along with the federal Green Book proposals in 1945–46, but not King. He did not feel the country was ready for new leaps in the direction of building a national character or "identity," so there was no new flag, no Canadian anthem, no attempts at patriation of the BNA Act. Indeed, if King ever thought about such things at all he would doubtless have considered them to be divisive. At best (or worst) he would have confided his thoughts to his famous diary — as he did, for example, when he compared the British Beveridge Report to his own *Industry and Humanity*. These night thoughts, however, never served as a guide to public policy. There was, in fact, only one potentially controversial initiative, the creation of Canadian citizenship in 1947 (up until then, Canadians had simply been British subjects), but even that turned out to be innocuous.

Louis St. Laurent, who became prime minister in 1948, was in many ways a very different man from King. But in the all-important area of how each looked upon the exercise of state power in Canada, they were similar. St. Laurent's biographer has characterized him as being "more interested in working out practical solutions to immediate problems than in devising utopic ones," and his career as prime minister bears this out. A nationalist in the Laurier sense (Laurier was, not surprisingly, his political hero), St. Laurent moved Canada a short distance farther along the road to full independence from Britain. In 1949 he ended all appeals from Canadian courts to the Judicial Committee of the Privy Council, and in 1952 he arranged the appointment of the first Canadian-born governor-general, Vincent Massey. He also sought the admission of Newfoundland to Canada, thus being the last prime minister to add territory to the country. But there were no efforts at constitutional reform or patriation under St. Laurent, there was no proposal for a new Canadian flag, there were no grandiose visions of some "new" Canada handed down from the lofty perch of Parliament Hill. In short, St. Laurent continued King's prudent avoidance of what might be called symbolic politics, the kind of political and rhetorical initiatives that fill one's life with "meaning" and public virtue but that carry a heavy cost that others down the road have to pay. Like King, St. Laurent was happy to allow Canadians to find their own meanings in life — in worship, in advancing their family position, in pursuing a career in plastics. The immediate postwar Liberal governments, in short, were also liberal in the sense established in chapter 1. St. Laurent's chief intention in matters domestic was to allow his very competent ministers to administer well and to keep the books in healthy balance. The search for "meaning" and virtue was a private affair for every Canadian.

It may be said that it was easy to run a country that had ample natural resources to sell to a market (primarily the United States) that had great need of them. That was certainly true of Canada in the years from the end of World War Two to the late 1950s. But there was also a clear philosophy of government behind the successes of the St. Laurent years. Foreign investment was welcomed as a necessary component of Canadian economic development. Prudent budgeting would keep taxes at reasonable levels and the national debt at a manageable proportion of the GNP. The government had entered an agreement with the International Monetary Fund to ensure that the value of the Canadian dollar was pegged.

The business of the government was the expansion of business opportunities for Canadian or foreign entrepreneurs and the development of such infrastructure — for example, pipelines — as was necessary. The government had no business moulding or shaping a Canadian character or creating and sustaining anything so vague as "social justice." Or perhaps it would be more accurate to say that the King legacy was that he kept the Government of Canada out of such things. But the King legacy was dwindling.

In the last years of the St. Laurent era, perhaps in response to opposition complaints that budgetary surpluses were too high and that the government had an obligation to share the wealth with the Canadian people, the Liberal administration initiated two measures that were clear departures from the spirit of the King reforms of the mid-1940s. The first was the introduction of equalization payments to the provinces; the second was the extension of unemployment insurance to fishermen.

The story of the genesis of regional equalization is too complex and too interconnected with the long development of federal-provincial tax-rental and revenue-sharing agreements to go into in any detail here. The result, however, was to create a system of fiscal federalism whereby Ottawa attempted to "equalize" the standards of basic and then not-so-basic services across Canada by paying money to "poor" or unproductive provinces or, subsequently, to poor or unproductive Canadians who, generally speaking, lived in poor and unproductive provinces. When, for example, the equalization payments that an unproductive province receives are added to the taxes that are raised in that province, the total amount will be roughly equal on a per capita basis to the revenues available to productive provinces. Because poor provinces are unproductive, their tax base is bound to be smaller, and the opposite is true for the productive provinces. The money paid to the "poor" provinces comes from Ottawa's general revenues and is transferred unconditionally so that it can be used for virtually anything by the provinces that receive it. Ottawa's general revenues, of course, are raised from all provinces. This means, in effect, that the productive provinces are transferring revenue to the unproductive ones, with Ottawa serving as the automatic banking machine. Currently, British Columbia, Alberta, and Ontario receive no equalization grants; all the other provinces do.

St. Laurent's government initiated equalization because, in the words of his biographer D.C. Thompson, "he ... felt that the federal government had a responsibility to see that Canadians had access to a comparable level of government services, in whatever province they lived." In other words, St. Laurent believed that all provinces ought to enjoy comparable revenues regardless of how much tax money they could raise from their own people. Sharing and caring are, without question, noble values. Moreover, there is a real joy to be found in generosity and in exercising the virtue of liberality. Such experiences and such virtues, however, belong to individuals. Considered as the expression of public virtue, liberality is a bad idea, the first step down the very slippery slope that leads to massive wealth redistribution undertaken with the aim of helping people in poorer areas of Canada but actually creating disincentives to work or relocate. It has been suggested that St. Laurent rationalized his policy on the basis of the extreme hardships he had seen in western Canada when he had travelled there in the late 1930s as general counsel for the Rowell-Sirois Commission. At the time he had been unable to do much to alleviate the misery he witnessed, and self-help schemes undertaken by the provinces — such as the Social Credit experiments in Alberta — were ruled unconstitutional by the courts and viewed by most Canadians outside Alberta as simply crackpot.

One can, therefore, understand why St. Laurent wished to take the initiative. It remains true, nevertheless, that the road Canadians have travelled to the present-day fiscal and economic morass has been paved with good intentions. None of those intentions was as thoughtlessly realized as regional equalization. First, the concept of equalization is moral, not economic. The history of economic growth is the history of men and women searching for ways to be more productive and more efficient with their labour and their resources. Any program that tells them that they need not search too hard because their living standards won't suffer too much if they are not successful, any program that tells people that their schools, hospitals, roads, and so on, will be kept up to a Canada-wide standard no matter how much unemployment there may be in the area is a disincentive to become productive and a disincentive to become more efficient. To be more precise, no provincial politician needs to be overly concerned with basic economic questions, such as how to live within a province's capacity to pay, if he or she knows that basic services will be paid for by somebody else. Instead of finding ways to change a poor and unproductive province into a more self-sufficient one, politicians from such provinces develop great skill at extracting concessions and at spending other people's money. Moreover, even if a politician is successful in diverting large amounts of money from the productive provinces to his or her own economic backwater, the result will be even greater dependence. Some politicians have developed very successful careers by diverting money in this way, and it is clearly in their short-term and individual interest to do so. But the point remains: they are increasing the dependency of their provinces, not their equality. In short, regional equalization payments can *never* lead to regional equality. They are, accordingly, perverse and a major contributing factor to the economic mess Canada is in.

The other big mistake that the St. Laurent government made

was to undermine the basic principle behind Canada's unemployment insurance scheme. Today Canada has a welfare program that is called "Unemployment Insurance" but that bears no more resemblance to real insurance than an apple does to a watermelon. When Canada's UI system was designed and implemented through a constitutional amendment in 1940, it was supposed to be supported by contributions from employers and employees, as well as by the federal government, and it was intended to be actuarially sound. In other words, the level of contributions was designed to create a self-sustaining fund in which there would be a surplus of money when unemployment was low to be drawn against when unemployment grew. There was no intention — and there was no mandate — to create a sinkhole that would be actuarially unsound, always out of balance, and that could be maintained only through massive and growing transfers of money from the federal government's general revenues to the UI fund. But that is exactly what has happened. In areas of Canada where population levels are simply too high to be sustained by the local economy, UI became a federally operated welfare program, known colloquially as Lotto 10/42: work for ten weeks a year, then collect UI for the remaining forty-two. Now people must work for twelve weeks before collecting; this is the revolutionary change introduced by Finance Minister Paul Martin in February 1994. The federal department of finance declared in a pamphlet published in January, 1994: "our UI system contains important disincentives to work." Indeed it does. But so too do equalization payments to provinces.

UI's downfall started in 1950 when the St. Laurent government first allowed a small number of seasonal workers to qualify for UI payments. This was an obvious contradiction in terms, because if work is seasonal then so too is the absence of work. And if one is bound to be unemployed there is no misfortune to be insured against, but an inevitability. No insurance company would ever extend insurance coverage to a person who inevitably will collect. That is why, for example, you cannot commit suicide in order to have your family benefit from your life insurance. The greatest blow to the integrity of UI came in 1956 when Jack Pickersgill, minister of fisheries and MP representing the Newfoundland riding of Bonavista-Twillingate, convinced his cabinet colleagues and a reluctant St. Laurent that self-employed fishermen should be allowed to qualify for UI. As he says in his memoirs: "I decided I could not face the electors of Bonavista-Twillingate again unless fishermen were covered." The opposition, not surprisingly, were delighted, as Pickersgill later recorded: "The decision was welcomed by spokesmen for all three opposition parties." And yet, it is absolutely certain that fishermen will not be fishing for large parts of the year. If this is turned into insurable unemployment, the economic, moral, and political principle upon which UI was based has been changed so that it bears no recognizable relation to the original purposes of the scheme. And why did this happen? Because Pickersgill, like St. Laurent before him, was "compassionate." And like St. Laurent, he forgot that compassion, if it is a virtue at all, is an individual not a political one.

Of course, Jack Pickersgill did not simply make an error in his moral philosophy. He thought it would be a good short-term policy for him, his party, and his government. The evolution of UI is, therefore, perfectly intelligible in terms of ordinary party politics. One of the dynamics that operates constantly in the Canadian House of Commons is that no party with national aspirations wants to be seen to be less generous to one particular region or major voter group than to any other. Hence no one asked what would be the impact on the financial health of the UI fund of admitting a large class of self-employed workers whose jobs were largely seasonal in nature. Moreover, it is rare that any opposition party will rise in the House to challenge any action of any government that bestows major favours on a large area of Canada or a large group of Canadians. This is one of the reasons why all the federal parties represented in the House in the late 1980s and early 1990s supported both the Meech Lake and Charlottetown Accords, and why a generation earlier they were so eager to support Pickersgill's changes to the Unemployment Insurance Act.

There is one last point to be made before leaving the subject of UI. Although St. Laurent, Pickersgill, and the finance minister, Walter Harris, were careful men who took their responsibilities seriously as guardians of the public purse, they inadvertently helped engineer our current ruinous rates of unemployment. For decades Canada has harboured one of the highest ongoing national rates of unemployment among the western industrialized countries. It is consistently higher by at least 25 per cent than that of the United States, our chief trading partner. Our rate has climbed from an average of 4.2 per cent in the 1950s, to 5 per cent in the 1960s, 6.7 per cent in the 1970s, 9.3 per cent in the 1980s, and over 11 per cent so far in the 1990s. It is no coincidence that Canada's UI is far more generous than the U.S. version and one of the most generous among the western industrialized countries. Although most everyone prefers to work for a living if possible, there is simply no getting away from the fact that some people will go to greater lengths, make more personal sacrifices, and change more of their lives to do so than others. The more comfortable not working is made, the higher the rate of non-working will invariably be. The UI scheme is akin to regional equalization grants in that it provides incentives to individuals to become dependants in the same way that equalization payments turn provinces into dependants. The consequences in both instances are perverse.

The St. Laurent government bowed to the pursuit of virtue in one other precedent-setting way — it established the Canada Council in 1957; the bulk of the original funds came from succession duties earned from two very large private estates. The council's first chairman was former Liberal cabinet minister Brooke Claxton, a great champion of Canadian culture. The council's mandate was fairly broad — to use the interest earned from the endowments to support Canadian culture and learning. Formation of the council had first been recommended in 1951 by the Royal Commission on the Arts, Letters and Sciences, headed by Vincent Massey.

In the beginning there was nothing wrong with the Canada Council and the impetus behind it, and much that was right. Scholars, artists (in the broadest sense), and scientific researchers are rarely self-sustaining economically (at least initially), and most countries have non-market mechanisms to support both artistic and scientific work using combinations of public and private funds. Many of the top-rated cultural institutions Canadians enjoy today would not be here without the Canada Council. One of the reasons why the Canada Council was able to do such good work was that although the initial council was chosen with careful attention to political affiliation (even though Claxton wanted the council members to be non-partisan), it operated at arm's length from government. Claxton's council supported culture in Canada but never tried to define Canadian culture. That is, for Claxton, as for most of his contemporaries, culture was understood in terms of the highest and most universal criteria. They would have been mystified by the notion of street-corner or teenage culture. Teenagers hanging out on street corners or in malls would have been thought to be characterized precisely by their lack of culture.

In later years, the Canada Council depended more heavily on government support and less on its original endowment. Subsequently, the Social Sciences and Humanities Research Council (SSHRC) was reorganized as an arm of the government (during the Trudeau years) to fund research, as opposed to culture. The temptations for these agencies to define, and so to fund, what they consider to be "Canadian" have been difficult to resist and have not always been resisted successfully.

Brooke Claxton was sure that the expense associated with the establishment of the Canada Council in 1957 was a major reason why John Diefenbaker won the federal election that year. That was bizarre. By and large, the St. Laurent Liberals had provided good government. Despite giving in to temptation on equalization and unemployment insurance, they had mostly steered clear of trying to tell Canadians who they were or what they ought to be. Louis St. Laurent is not generally recognized by journalists or scholars as among Canada's "great" prime ministers, mostly because he was a transitional leader who probably should have retired just before or just after the 1953 election. But he shared one important trait with Macdonald, Laurier, and King — he understood the basic limits of state power that were imposed by the realities of the Confederation arrangement and he mostly steered clear of testing those limits. He and his ministers saw the initiation of equalization and the rejigging of UI as little more than extending the pragmatic social welfare state that the King government had already initiated. He and they did not initiate these moves as part of any campaign to promote public virtue through the operations of government. At the same time, however, the changes they made would provide opportunities for further expansion at the hands of their successors, who had quite a different agenda. The first of these was John George Diefenbaker.

Diefenbaker was Canada's first charismatic prime minister. Macdonald had been loved, Laurier had been respected, but neither one, indeed, no Canadian leader until that time, had aroused the Canadian people as Diefenbaker did. He did so not only with his barn-burning, prairie-populist speaking style but also with his message. After more than two decades of highly competent but boring administration from the Liberals, the Canadian people seemed to crave vision and challenge. The problem with vision and challenge in a country such as Canada is that there is rarely any consensus on what the vision should be and which challenges ought to be met. That bothered neither Diefenbaker nor the vast majority of the voters, who gave him his first taste of office in 1957, then swept him to power in 1958.

Diefenbaker came to power at the head of the Progressive Conservative party, but Diefenbaker was no conservative. Born in Ontario, he had moved west as a young boy and had been raised on a homestead in Saskatchewan. His politics and his political ideas were rooted in the soil of western protest and the Saskatchewan variant of prairie populism. He had virtually nothing in common with the by-the-bootstraps, ruggedly individual free enterprisers who had for decades dominated the Tory party. Diefenbaker, in common with many other western populists, believed government ought to be the great equalizer, that governments had a responsibility to establish a level playing field for all citizens, and that all citizens had a right to share in the opportunity for, and to some extent in the fruits of, national wealth creation. It followed that the national government had a responsibility to guard the interests of the downtrodden of society.

Populism in Canada, as in other countries, has been intimately linked to agrarian protest. It is a sufficiently broad term to include not only Diefenbaker but also the Progressives, the farmer parties in Alberta and Ontario, the CCF in Saskatchewan, Social Credit in Alberta, and, nowadays, the Reform party. There are clear differences between, for example, the CCF or its successor, the NDP, and the Reform party. But only a simple-minded preference for dividing the world into left and right allows us to overlook the fact that a wide range of populists share a critical assessment of certain aspects of the economy and the conventions governing Canadian political practice.

Diefenbaker was determined to change not only how the government of Canada operated, but also the country itself. He sought to undertake major renovations in the fabric of Canadian political life so that it more closely mirrored his view of the world and reflected more accurately his experiences and the aspirations of Canadians who shared those experiences. That marked a major difference with most of the Canadian governments that had preceded his. Leaders like Macdonald, Laurier, and King had steered clear of any effort to change the basic shape and nature of the very diverse country they were governing, but Diefenbaker leaped in with abandon. Where King and the others had known that their chief responsibility was to administer well while expanding economic opportunity, Diefenbaker believed that his chief responsibility was to change Canada according to his own vision, his ideological preconceptions if you like. Under King, and to a somewhat lesser degree St. Laurent, economic and social policy had been designed to achieve the ends of good government and the expansion of economic opportunities; under Diefenbaker, economic and social policy was designed to serve the kind of Canada Diefenbaker wanted to see emerge. He had a real agenda for change. The impact on the bottom line would be obvious soon enough: under Diefenbaker economic good sense would be sacrificed for so-called higher ideals. King, Macdonald, and most other prime ministers up to that day knew there was no higher public ideal that a Canadian national government could serve than economic good sense.

What sort of Canada did John Diefenbaker want to build? First of all, in his oft-quoted words of February 1958, it would be: "One Canada. One Canada, where Canadians will have preserved to them the control of their own economic and political destiny. Sir John A. Macdonald gave his life to this party. He opened the West. He saw Canada from east to west. I see a new Canada — a Canada of the North." Diefenbaker evoked a new sense of Canadian citizenship, greater independence from the United States, and an emphasis on northern development as an engine of economic growth and development. This last idea was generated by a now little known but rather remarkable Canadian thinker, Merril Warren Menzies. A specialist in Canadian agricultural economics with a PhD from the London School of Economics, Menzies had at one time served as executive assistant to Liberal justice minister Stuart Garson; he then offered his services to Diefenbaker. Menzies had written to Diefenbaker that "the Canadian people want ... *vision* in their statesmen, a sense of national purpose, and national destiny." He believed that where there was no vision, the people and the nation would perish. So he and Diefenbaker would give Canadians the vision that had apparently been missing from their national politics for years. Of course, Canadians didn't know what they had missed, but once it was pointed out to them, once the presence of an absence had entered their consciousness, they knew what they had to have. In short, the people swallowed Diefenbaker's vision thing whole.

Diefenbaker's northern vision eventually produced some highways, some railway track, and some expanded government services in the north. But little else. The simple reality is that there isn't much in the Canadian north that will sustain a large population and, in the absence of compelling disincentives, people generally are ready to move if they think they will gain socially or economically by doing so. Diefenbaker's Northern Vision was a catchy vote-getter and provided a good deal of the vision hoopla that Menzies (and the voters) craved, but it had little substance. And when the country became mired in an economic downturn shortly after Diefenbaker took office, Canadians' attention turned to more mundane matters, like jobs.

Diefenbaker's Canada, then, was to be a "nation of the north" (shades of Canada First!). It was also to be a country where ethnic or religious or linguistic roots were to be subordinated to a single citizenship. Canadians would become "unhyphenated" in thought, word, and deed, if Diefenbaker had anything to say about it. Here, too, was a way of looking at the country that was directly rooted in his personal experience. As one whose antecedents were neither "English" nor "French" (as was the case with several million other western Canadians) he had grown up believing that good Canadians remained proud of their forebears but came together in the present without regard to race, language, religion, and so on. In this respect Diefenbaker's views were identical with those of Tommy Douglas and Preston Manning. This shared perception was a central element of their common populism.

The essence of Diefenbaker's "One Canada" philosophy was his Bill of Rights, introduced in 1960. It was only a federal statute, not entrenched in the constitution, and it thus could be changed at any time by Parliament and had no impact on provincial legislation. But it neatly embodied his view of the world. One might have asked: just what is an unhyphenated Canadian, Mr. Diefenbaker? And he would likely have answered: "the Parliament of Canada has now defined Canadian citizens on the basis of the rights bestowed upon them by the Canadian Bill of Rights."

Diefenbaker apparently ignored the fact that a bill or a government that bestows rights can also remove them. He surely ignored the accumulated wisdom of Western liberal democracy, which declares that the purpose of government is to *secure* the rights of citizens that exist by nature, that is, *prior* to any legislation.

Diefenbaker's unhyphenated Canadians were also going to be more collectively independent than they had been in the past. This meant independent of the United States. One of the silliest of the many silly things that Diefenbaker promised to do — a promise that reveals much about the manner in which he subordinated economic common sense to ideological goals — was to divert 15 per cent of Canada's import trade from the United States to the United Kingdom. The British government apparently took this promise seriously, because it offered to establish an Anglo-Canadian free trade area in which tariffs would be eliminated over a fifteen-year period. Diefenbaker never really followed up on the British offer and it disappeared into thin air. Even by then Canadians had evolved a strong trading relationship with the United States; efforts to block or divert Canada-U.S. trade were as doomed to failure as efforts to amend the laws of gravity.

Diefenbaker's Canada was going to be a society founded upon social justice, not a society that offered its citizens social welfare when they needed it. This built upon the groundwork that the St. Laurent Liberals had begun, but Diefenbaker took it much farther. In a 1960 article in *Maclean's* magazine, Peter C. Newman put it this way: "Diefenbaker has claimed to be giving Canadians help that it is their right to *expect*. He talks always of social justice, never of social welfare. It's social welfare to get help when you need it; it's social justice to be brought up to the same economic level as your `fellow Canadians' for a chance to compete in this country's development." Diefenbaker, then, never accepted the basic

assumption of both liberals and conservatives in modern society —
that it is morally wrong and economically unsound for individuals
to become dependent upon the state for their personal prosperity.
As he himself put it in a 1961 speech: "every man, woman and
child in the nation has the right as a citizen — indeed, as one of
the co-owners of most of the land and most of the resources still
... 'vested in the Crown' — ... to a share in the national progress
and prosperity." Thus Canadian wealth, having been based on the
exploitation of the resources that all citizens owned in common,
was something that all Canadians had a right to share in. Diefenbaker's populism took on a distinctly communitarian coloration.

In putting his brand of populism into policy, Diefenbaker laid
the groundwork for the Pearson and Trudeau eras that followed.
He introduced the notion that, if citizens were not doing well, or
thought they were not doing well enough, the efforts of government to distribute their share of the national wealth to them must
be redoubled. If citizens did not enjoy an equal standard of services wherever they might live, it was government's responsibility
to see to it that bad or "substandard" services were improved. If
intelligent, courageous, and ambitious citizens did well, it was government's task to take an increasing share of the fruits of their
labour from them and give it to those who, for whatever reason,
were not doing so well. It was an extraordinary philosophy, especially for a Tory, and it planted the seeds of subsequent economic
disaster. The reason was simple: first of all, there is not enough
money on the face of the earth, let alone in Canada, for any government to redress the inherent inequality of talent, brains, initiative, courage, and ability that differentiates people from one
another everywhere. Nor is there enough money to put fish back
into the sea when there are no fish, or to keep Cape Breton coal in
demand as a valuable resource when the rest of the world has

found alternative sources of energy. And even if it were not simply a matter of scarce resources, the fact remains that, as Aristotle pointed out some time ago, treating unequals equally is as unjust as treating equals unequally. Neither Diefenbaker nor his ministers seemed to acknowledge either the problem of limited resources or the consequent necessity to moderate desires. Alternatively, if they did consider costs, they were swept away by the belief that no burden was too great to bear in the pursuit of a socially just society. And finally, Diefenbaker and his government were utterly oblivious to the home truth that when governments do things for their citizens, rather than allow them to do things on their own, which means allowing them to succeed *and* to fail, they turn them into dependants, pure and simple.

Although Diefenbaker's government introduced very few new spending programs (hospital insurance was the exception), it spent much more on existing programs than previous governments had done. Diefenbaker expanded equalization payments, and turned the nation into a crazy patchwork of special social and economic subsidies. Alberta had oil resources that were too expensive for consumers in Ontario? Divide the nation at the Ottawa River according to the recommendations of a royal commission and reserve the Ontario market for Alberta oil. Atlantic Canada was suffering from chronic unemployment? Rejig equalization and provide special tax incentives for industry to locate in Atlantic Canada. And on and on it went.

The pattern was clear. Welfare payments increased by roughly 100 per cent during the Diefenbaker era, and about 80 per cent of the people of Canada received some form of direct government assistance in the form of family allowances, old age security, and other programs. Canadians became a nation of pensioners. In areas of chronic unemployment such as Atlantic Canada, people came to depend on "the pogey" for their very existence. The once-sound UI fund melted away. Payments were expanded and eligibility rules relaxed; equalization payments were placed on a different, and higher, plane.

Now, it is certainly true that the Diefenbaker government had a recession to fight and true also that, according to classical Keynesian theory, it was doing some of the right things to fight that deficit with winter works programs and generous welfare payouts. But the increases in government spending during the Diefenbaker years were not simply driven by economic need. They were linked closely to Diefenbaker's notion of what Canada was supposed to be as a nation, and were intended to change the basis on which citizens related to each other and to their government. It was no coincidence that the first government in Canadian history to attempt to implement an a priori definition of Canada and Canadians was also the first government run by a charismatic prime minister and the first government to accept the notion that it had a direct responsibility to guarantee social justice to its citizens. Diefenbaker and his finance ministers did not deliberately eschew sound and prudent fiscal and economic management. They strongly believed they were being no less responsible than the leaders who had preceded them. But what they did do — and knowingly — was to place objectives such as the achievement of social justice at the top of the government's agenda. Social justice, a version of what we earlier called public virtue, became the end; economic management became the means to achieve it. They either did not know, or they refused to believe, that social justice meant collectivism pure and simple.

The argument is simple and is known to every student who takes an introductory course in political science. For liberals, in the sense that we used the term in chapter 1, justice is essentially what it was in the Roman Code of Justinian: "a firm and unceasing determination to render everyone his or her due." *Equal* justice under law means that all holdings, large and small, are protected and the right to hold one's own is secured by law. This understanding of justice says nothing about the size of one's own or what is one's due. *Social* justice, as Dickerson and Flanagan pointed out in their text, *An Introduction to Government and Politics*, concerns not the protection or securing of one's own but a distribution of everyone's holdings that conforms to a previously chosen target. Social justice almost invariably means using the state to intervene in the otherwise free action of human beings in order to secure equal outcomes or, as is sometimes said, *more* equal outcomes.

It is simply inevitable that when demands arise from political leaders or elsewhere to enforce social justice, property and wealth will be taken from those who have more and given to those who have less. So far as liberal individualists are concerned, the correct term for social justice is theft. It violates the freedom of the productive in order to enhance the dependency of the unproductive. There is, accordingly, a net loss of freedom for everyone, both the unwilling benefactors and the alleged beneficiaries. Obviously, social justice has nothing in common with using the state to provide collective goods such as law and order, harbours, roads, or even scientific research: collective goods may restrict the freedom of all, because they are paid for by taxes, but such restrictions are for the benefit of all. Social justice benefits no one but the bureaucrats who administer the policies that put this perverse objective into practice.

Social justice was not the only fuzzy target Diefenbaker aimed at that threw Canada's economy off balance. Another was his embrace of a peculiar kind of patriotism, which we now call Cana-

dian nationalism. Starting with his bizarre idea that he could simply wave a magic wand and change Canada-U.S. trade flows,
Diefenbaker seemed determined to strengthen Canadians' national
self-esteem. The way we would know we were a free and independent people was by criticizing and opposing the United States.
Not since the 1911 reciprocity election had a Canadian prime minister built so much of his political reputation on tweaking Uncle
Sam's nose. Yet things were very different in the late 1950s than
they had been in 1911; by Diefenbaker's time, Canada had become
much more closely tied to the United States financially, economically, and in matters of trade, defence, and foreign policy. The
backroom strategists within the Tory hierarchy thought that running against the United States was the one tactic that might bring
positive electoral results when Diefenbaker once again sought a
mandate.

There is nothing at all wrong with love of country, and the
argument has often been made that Canadians have, if anything,
too little of it. But there is a difference between a love of country
that emerges from the experience of lives individually lived by
Canadians and the creation of a politically motivated nationalism
based on criticism of other countries. In Canada, when anti-Amer-
icanism begins to move policy, one can be pretty confident that
those who promote it, including governments, have gone off the
rails. In a very real sense every Canadian prime minister from
Macdonald's time to the present day has seen his or her role as
that of guardian of Canadian national independence, however that
was defined. But the Diefenbaker government went that one step
farther; it began to make decisions not on the basis of what it perceived to *be* in the national interest, but in pursuit of its own ideal
of what a Canadian nationalism *ought* to consist of. The chief aim
of the national government under Diefenbaker was no longer

what we have called economic fundamentalism but the promulgation of Diefenbaker's brand of Canadianism.

Even that would have been fine if his brand of Canadianism had represented some national consensus reached after decades of Canadians' growing together; but it did not. The narrowness of Diefenbaker's vision became clearly apparent after June 1960, when the Quebec Liberal party under Jean Lesage launched the so-called Quiet Revolution.

Much has been written, by us in *Deconfederation*, and by others, about the Quiet Revolution and the response to it inside and outside French Canada. We do not intend to repeat it all here. We do want to point out, however, that just as Diefenbaker in effect broke faith with Canadians by trying to convince them that it was appropriate for them to pursue a vision of public virtue in national politics, Lesage broke faith with those of his fellow Canadians who lived outside Quebec (and many who lived inside it) by trying to convince them that they owed it to him and to themselves to re-examine the bases upon which the nation was founded. As we have argued, however, there never was and there is not now any such need. When Diefenbaker decided to add the role of national cheerleader to all the other tasks he wanted the national government to perform, he abandoned the search for good government in favour of the search for collective virtue. In launching his Quiet Revolution, Lesage did the same.

During and after Diefenbaker's term as prime minister, the question was often raised as to whether or not Dief the Chief "understood" Quebec. Certainly he offered only token changes in the direction of greater bilingualism (with such measures as bilingual federal cheques), and his government suffered badly for his failure to establish political roots in Quebec. We believe, however, that people have consistently raised questions about Diefenbaker that were based on faulty assumptions. Specifically, they have assumed that by responding differently, or with more "understanding," he might have mitigated the more extreme forms of Quebec nationalism that took shape during his time. And by asking for more "understanding" of Quebec, Diefenbaker's critics mean that he should have agreed to just about anything Lesage and his supporters demanded. But the real question, we think, should have been: "Why respond at all?" Why did Diefenbaker need to react to the Quiet Revolution in any special manner?

In our view Diefenbaker should have delivered a clear message that when Quebec acted within its already ample jurisdiction (ample in that all the provinces of Canada have a wide range of powers), the province was perfectly within its rights to carry out whatever reforms it wished. At the same time, another message should have indicated that although the political arrangements underlying matters such as tax-rental agreements were always open for discussion, no discussion of the essential constitutional bargain of 1867 would be entertained. To do so would mean plunging into the murky waters of attempting to redefine Canada and Canadians and posing an acute threat to the national consensus. But that message of prudence was not sent. Dief gave neither a clear "yes" nor a clear "no" to Quebec. He responded positively to Quebec's suggestion that justice minister E. Davie Fulton should attempt to work out an agreement between Ottawa and the provinces for an amending formula to precede patriation of the constitution. But he said little or nothing when Quebec eventually rejected the Fulton formula because it did not offer to transfer Unemployment Insurance to provincial jurisdiction. In fact, that refusal was simply the first of many attempted power grabs by Quebec.

In all that Diefenbaker did in the way of social justice, and in much that he did in other matters, he had the strong support of the opposition Liberals. Were the Liberals going to complain when Diefenbaker increased welfare, equalization, and other entitlement payments? Were they going to handicap their vote-getting ability in the West, for example, by criticizing the government's energy program, or shoot themselves in the foot in Atlantic Canada by attacking subsidies for relocating industry? Once again the political system ensured that there would be no brakes on the government's actions. The only question debated was how much money Ottawa ought to shovel out to individuals and to provinces and not whether Diefenbaker's notion of social justice made sense or was desirable. In effect, both Conservatives and Liberals agreed on the desirability of social justice, collective virtue, and communitarianism. One need look no farther to see the real beginnings of what went wrong.

The Liberals regained power with a minority government under Lester Pearson in April 1963, but they had begun to think about these questions several years earlier. The process began in September 1960, at a Liberal think-tank held in Kingston, and continued in January 1961 with a giant Liberal "Rally" held to discuss policy. It was there that Pearson's Liberal government first took shape under the guiding hand of former newspaperman Tom Kent and long-time Pearson political crony and supporter, accountant Walter Gordon.

In 1948 Gordon had helped put together a trust fund that would allow Lester Pearson to leave the civil service and enter politics. In 1958 he had organized Pearson's leadership campaign. In 1963 he became Pearson's first minister of finance after helping to engineer the Liberal victory. He was a man of considerable influence in the Pearson government, and he retained much of that influence even after a falling out with Pearson.

Walter Gordon strongly believed in activist government and was convinced that the Government of Canada had a duty to mould, shape, and direct the development of the Canadian national character and thereby promote public virtue. He wanted Ottawa to control the flow of foreign investment into Canada, particularly American investment, and the federal government to direct private savings into investments in Canadian enterprises. He was determined, on the one hand, to enhance the power of the central government, but on the other he was willing to concede that Quebec was not a province like the others and had special requirements. He strongly supported the view that Canada is "a bilingual nation" comprised of "two distinct societies with different languages and cultures" and that one of those cultures was centred in the province of Quebec. Considered simply as a kind of loose sociological description of Canada, few would quarrel with Gordon's observations. Gordon, however, was not concerned with sociology but with real-world political decisions and political deals. For him the political consequences were clear: he wanted the national government to take the lead in developing "more symbols, more traditions, and more in the way of clearly identifiable policies to remind [Canadians] of their country and the pride they should take in it." Here was a cook with a recipe for disaster. Symbols convey meanings born of real experiences; they are not logos invented by governments to make people feel good. Traditions, literally, are handed down from generation to generation in a myriad of small ways, through family and local stories, public celebrations of significant collective acts, and so forth; they are not the products of government public-relations campaigns. Any government or political party that conceives its task to be that of telling citizens what they should take pride in has mistaken the purpose of government for that of an ad campaign. In sum, Gordon went

Diefenbaker one better in advocating that Ottawa ought to be the national cheerleader, even though there was no evidence that Canadians would ever agree on which cheer they wanted to hear. Walter Gordon wanted to bring the pursuit of collective public virtue to the centre of Canadian national politics.

Gordon's nationalism went hand in glove with Tom Kent's economic interventionism. The main components of Kent's program, first laid out at the Kingston meeting, were: (1) medicare; (2) sickness insurance (which he defined as "the same level of income-maintenance for sick people as for those who are unemployed for other reasons"); (3) the revamping of UI to make it "also a protection against disaster" (in other words, in the event that unemployment was prolonged, there would be a high level of income maintenance subject to a willingness to accept job mobility and undertake training); (4) extensive manpower training; (5) regional development ("Government should moderate adjustments by public investments and inducements to move some jobs to where the workers are"); (6) urban renewal; (7) more public housing; (8) better schools; (9) increased federal aid to universities and university students; (10) enhanced social services through federal assistance to provinces, municipalities, and voluntary agencies; (11) enhanced foreign aid. Kent later claimed he was not "building a federal political platform" at Kingston, but in fact much of what he laid out was endorsed at the Liberal Rally, became part of the 1962 and 1963 Liberal election platforms, and formed the basis of the Pearson legislative program.

It was all pretty Utopian, and there is some evidence, at least, that it did not go down well with St. Laurent, now the party's grand old man. For the then seventy-nine-year-old former prime minister, the chief hallmark of a Liberal government was good administration, not dreamy ideals. Instead of promising better administration, as King had done when out of power in the Great Depression, Pearson's opposition Liberals were going to promise a better world for all Canadians. It was Diefenbaker's social justice taken much farther than its originator had ever dared. No one seemed seriously to have asked how the national treasury was going to pay for all this. But then, that was only an accounting detail. For those Pearsonian Liberals who were determined to shape a better Canada — and a better Canadian — the price, whatever it turned out to be, was acceptable. The sixties were to be a decade of prosperity; once the Diefenbaker recession had been thrown off it was going to be onward and upward for all.

The Pearson years were marked by three major trends: increased nationalism in Ottawa's economic decision making (even after Gordon departed from Finance); economic interventionism; and the launching of the Royal Commission on Bilingualism and Biculturalism, known widely as the Bi-Bi Commission — and among cynics as the bye-bye commission: Quebec was saying bye-bye to Canada. Each of these initiatives has been written about in great detail elsewhere, but some brief explanation is required here.

The nationalism of the Pearson government was expressed primarily in legislation such as the anti-American investment stipulations of the early Gordon budgets, in the establishment of the Canada Development Corporation, in the new Canadian flag (1964), and in the ballyhoo leading up to and during the centennial celebrations of 1967. Some of these measures, many Canadians agreed, were well past due, especially the new Canadian flag. But taken together with the rest of the government's legislative agenda, they represented a disturbing tendency to tell Canadians what "Canadianism" was supposed to mean.

The Pearson government leaned heavily towards economic

interventionism in a number of ways. First, it greatly expanded the scope of the Canadian welfare state with the introduction of the Canada Pension Plan (1966), medicare (1968), and significant increases in social welfare spending. In principle, the concepts involved may well have been sound, but in the case of medicare, at least, a program was launched with open-ended spending possibilities. It all seemed so simple, at the time — tell the provinces that they would receive substantial federal funds if they launched provincial plans that were universal, comprehensive, portable, and accessible. But no one considered the consequences for the whole scheme as the population aged and new technologies made advanced medicine more and more expensive. It seemed that, with childlike optimism, the Pearsonian Liberals assumed they could do just about anything, and the future be damned. Perhaps even worse, they hoped the future would take care of itself.

The government also gave federal public service workers the right to strike and was promptly struck by seaway workers, postal workers, air traffic controllers, and others, who fought for and won major wage increases, contributing to the wage-driven inflation of the early 1970s. It poured hundreds of millions of dollars into regional development schemes, especially for the Atlantic region, and it used the institution of the Crown corporation (as in Cape Breton) as a means of maintaining jobs in thoroughly unproductive areas. Through its actions the government declared, in essence, that "the public," which meant productive Canadians, had a responsibility to use Crown corporations to subsidize jobs that would not otherwise exist.

Finally, Pearson started Canada down the road to official bilingualism. The B & B Commission was established soon after Pearson came to power, and its recommendations have formed the backbone of Canadian language and cultural policy ever since.

Bilingualism was an answer to a question no one was asking. The nationalists inside the Quebec government did not care one iota about the fate of Francophone communities outside Quebec; they wanted more power for the Quebec provincial government or they wanted independence: they were not fighting for the right of Franco-Albertans to be told to buckle their seat belts in French. English-speaking Canadians outside Quebec usually had no need to learn French, and if they did, they took it upon themselves to do so, for business or professional reasons, much as they would learn German, Japanese, or Ugaritic. But once again the government operated on the assumption — an assumption that underlay much of what it did — that people are incapable of making the "right" choices and so governments must choose what is best for them.

Taken together, these Pearsonian policies pointed in the direction that the Liberal party thought Canada ought to go in the future. First, Ottawa would eschew its one-time narrow approach to national administration and would now adopt holus-bolus the task that Canada First had once urged on Macdonald — the creation of a distinctive Canadian national character. Second, the creation of that national character would be at the top of the agenda, and everything else would be subordinated to it. Third, the new Canadian character itself was going to be created in the image of the thinkers and doers that Pearson had collected around him. So, for example, Canada was going to be bilingual and bicultural whether or not it made sense of Canadian reality, whether or not the nation could afford it, whether or not it actually drew Canadians together. They would do so by making bilingualism and biculturalism part of the national creed and, by lifting it above politics, turn it into an expression of our collective public virtue. When the Tories decided in the mid-1970s that they would from now on select only a bilingual leader who supported bilingualism and biculturalism, the victory of the Pearsonian Liberals was complete. It was all top-down, the imposition of untested bright ideas, and a world away from the kind of government that Macdonald, Laurier, King, and even St. Laurent had provided. With Mike Pearson, Canada had a new kind of collectivist government ready, willing, and able to provide guarantees that various hitherto unknown "rights" could be exercised. For example, the combination of regional equalization and Crown corporations created the new "right" of, for example, a Cape Breton Islander to live where he was born whether or not there were any local jobs. Prior to the Pearson government's creation of this "right," the Cape Bretoner had the option of exercising the right to live in his home town, but the rest of the country did not have the obligation to provide him with a job.

Pearson, and the people of Canada, were fortunate that the money was clearly there to pay for it all, at least in the short run. The international demand for Canadian goods, especially but not exclusively raw materials, soared in the 1960s, and governments at all levels embarked on massive capital-improvement projects. As the baby boomers entered the workforce, better educated than any previous generation, they paid taxes by the billions. Once Gordon was out of Finance — he was, by all measures, a poor finance minister — and was replaced by the more traditional Mitchell Sharp, something approaching sanity was re-established in Canadian economic and fiscal policy. Sharp might have been a finance minister under King or St. Laurent, in that he believed in sound and prudent fiscal management. The real danger, however, lay in the future that the government was creating and that successive generations of taxpayers were going to have to pay for. Canada was being given an economic structure of subsidies, special tax

concessions, built-in unemployment benefits, equalization payments, social welfare measures, and disincentives to economic
mobility, all of which worked after a fashion when there was
money to throw around, but that would generate mountains of
debt after the party ended. It was a fool's paradise: Canada was
being given an economic structure that could not (and now does
not) work.

What was this new Canada going to look like? It would be
more nationalistic. It would be a country where all Canadians
would be deemed to have a share in the national wealth, by right,
regardless of what they had contributed. It would be a Canada
where government would be deemed capable of virtually anything, given sufficient "planning" (a key buzzword of the 1960s)
and unlimited resources. And it would be a Canada where people
were expected to fit into a preordained mould. Canadians would
be part of a "peaceable kingdom," they would be bilingual, they
would "understand" Quebec, they would be good citizens of the
world, they would not do nasty things such as participate in wars
or support those of their allies who did. They would do all this
under a new flag they ought to be proud of, and they would proclaim it to the world at their very own birthday party, Expo 67 in
Montreal, which marked the centennial of Confederation. It was
heady stuff, eagerly lapped up by an exultant people, but it was
also dangerous. And yet, the process of character moulding had
barely begun when Pearson left office at the end of Centennial
Year and turned the reins of power over to his successor, Pierre
Elliott Trudeau.

The conclusion to be drawn is this: by the end of the Diefen-
baker/Pearson era, Canadian politics had been transformed and
Canadian government had changed along with it. In the period
1957 to 1967 Diefenbaker and Pearson (and their advisers and

ministers) had redefined the role of the national government. Henceforth that role was not simply to administer, but to create and shape and mould a national character and, above all, to pursue collective public virtue. Caution and careful administration had fallen by the wayside. To use the language of the day, Canada had "come of age." It found in Pierre Trudeau a leader who expressed the new sentiments, believed them to be nothing less than the rational truth, and had the energy, intelligence, and ruthlessness to act on his beliefs. His would be the high tide of the search for collective public virtue and easily the administration most damaging to the economic fundamentalism that had once enabled Canada to prosper.

4
Towards
the Higher
Mendacity

A recent biography of Pierre Elliott Trudeau opened with the abrupt declaration: "He haunts us still." This is hyperbole. Trudeau is, in fact, not a ghost but a prosperous Montreal lawyer, and few Canadians nowadays give him much of their waking or sleeping attention. Yet the hyperbole contains a truth: Trudeau's policies have outlasted his administration and they do, indeed, have an impact on every living Canadian and on Canadians yet unborn.

One key to why Trudeau has had such lasting importance can be found in a collection of self-serving essays, *Towards a Just Society*, written by important members of what René Lévesque used to call "the Trudeau gang." In their introductory remarks, Trudeau and Tom Axworthy declare: "Make no mistake, we were an ideological government — ideological in the sense that we were motivated by an overarching framework of purpose ... we tried to be a government of ideas." Indeed.

The novelty of the Trudeau government was not that it had a purpose, for every government demonstrates its purposes through its public policies. Rather it was that its purpose was conceived as an "idea" and, what was probably even more unusual, the Trudeau gang thought that their "ideas" elevated their purposes. Historian Michael Bliss has characterized Trudeau as a "fighting intellectual" and considers the type to be a rare and puzzling kind of human being. Perhaps so: but considered in political terms, fighting intellectuals promise immoderate politics.

Intellectuals brimming with bright ideas usually operate on the political margins — in churches, universities, or the media — so they can't do too much damage to the body politic. Moreover, they can be distinguished from priests, scholars, and old-fashioned reporters, as well as from practical men and women of affairs by their warm attachment to ideas and their lack of (and lack of appreciation for) common sense. But common sense, or to give this quality a more lofty name, prudence, is the first requirement of a decent politician. Mackenzie King, to take an obvious example, was as intellectually gifted as Trudeau, but he was also prudent. It is true that his private spiritual life was distinctly odd and his one book, *Industry and Humanity*, was a strange patchwork of opinions, but neither had much impact on his political judgement. The same cannot be said of Trudeau and his associates. They did truly fancy themselves as intellectuals in politics.

In any case, Trudeau the individual and Trudeau the politician were just as much at odds as was the internally divided Mackenzie King, whose "very double life" has quite properly been a source of scholarly wonder. As his *Memoirs* make clear, Trudeau has relished from the days of his youth playing the iconoclastic prankster and taking up contrarian poses to enjoy the effect on those of more conventional habits. "The only constant factor to be found in my thinking," Trudeau wrote by way of introducing himself to English readers of *Federalism and the French Canadians*, "has been opposition to accepted opinions.... I have never been able to accept any discipline except that which I imposed upon myself ... I found it unacceptable that others should claim to know better than I what was good for me."

The political or public expression of this blend of Left Bank existentialism and dilettantish self-advertising has been a montage of evocative but hardly coherent images: Trudeau played the gunslinger, alone on stage like Dirty Harry or Josey Wales, tie loosened, jacket off, fingers hooked in his belt loops; Trudeau took on the terrorists in the FLQ by invoking the War Measures Act and challenged his "bleeding heart" critics to "just watch" how far he would go; Trudeau changed the constitution in his own image, taking on the gang of eight premiers, the Supreme Court of Canada, and the Parliament of Great Britain; Trudeau, the champion of "renewed federalism," rode into the lists against René Lévesque and the Péquistes in the longest-running soap-opera in the history of Quebec; Trudeau removed the state from the bedrooms of the nation and struck a blow for easier divorce, easier access to abortion, and what today would be called gay liberation; Trudeau scandalized the blue-suit brigade when he showed up in Parliament in sandals and an ascot; he drove an ageing Porsche, like himself in mint condition, dated beautiful young women in New York and took them scuba diving in Tahiti; then he topped off his gay bachelor life by wedding an apparently radiant flower child from British Columbia. Strenuous training at the hands of Jesuits and judo masters enhanced his stance of tough individualism. Probably the most expressive image of the man, repeated in several contexts, and most recently in the TV miniseries celebrating his life, is labelled "lone-man-in-a-canoe." Here we see him, garbed in buckskin, gliding silently through the water with an occasional effortless paddle stroke. The message of the icon is clear: Pierre, the *voyageur*, paddled his own canoe, indifferent to the camera, steely glint in his eye. One cannot help noting, as he disappears around the bend with his back to those stranded on shore, that he has been paddling with the current.

Trudeau's loudly proclaimed individualism, if that is what it was, contained its opposite in the public man. He was a man who would try to use the state to give Canadians things — rights and freedoms, for example. Apparently, somewhere along the line, he forgot that such things simply are not in the gift of the state. He must have forgotten this lesson from liberalism, because surely, in his much celebrated exposure to genuinely great minds at Harvard, the LSE and the Sorbonne, he would have learned that simple truth. Along the way he also gave us massive amounts of welfare and a ruined economy, two forms of corruption that are often associated.

The paradox of a self-proclaimed individualist who promotes state action to ensure that rights are enforced is another version of the paradox of the "fighting intellectual." In Trudeau we can see the problem, which we have called bad government or the promotion of collective public virtue, writ small in the actions of a man who holds the view that, as he said with great candour in his *Memoirs*, "the role of the federal government is to distribute wealth from the affluent to the disadvantaged."

It is a curious position for one such as Trudeau to take. Pierre Trudeau is a wealthy Liberal, but thinks that the role of the state is to distribute (or redistribute) wealth, necessarily including his own wealth, to the poor, whom he calls disadvantaged. Pierre Trudeau is a "fighting intellectual," and Liberal intellectuals, whether they are bellicose or pacifist, are a minority, and yet they promote democracy and policies that help the disadvantaged. Wealthy fighting intellectuals cannot be unaware of their own advantages. They must know that, by promoting the interests of the disadvantaged, they are not promoting their own interests either as wealthy persons (for most people are not wealthy) or as fighters (for most people are not ambitious enough to fight) or as intellectuals (for most people are not clever). So: why do they do it?

The answer, as Harvey Mansfield has discovered, is that liberal fighting intellectuals take pride in promoting interests other than their own. As Trudeau himself remarked in his *Memoirs*: "I always thought the role of the state, and my role as a politician, was to speak for those who had no voice." When people such as Trudeau become aware of what they are doing, which, because they are clever as well as ambitious and wealthy, does not take them very long, their pride is redoubled. "For," Mansfield said, "pride takes pride in rising above interest." Now conscious of having risen above their own interests, fighting intellectuals such as Trudeau become earnest, loving, and generous taxpayers, or at least they insist that the rest of us do so. The difficulty and the source of the bad faith at the heart of such a position is that the disadvantaged never get a chance to exercise their own rights and take pride in their own achievements. Trudeau "always thought" his role was to speak for the voiceless, but who put that thought into his head? Certainly not the voiceless. In order for Trudeau to speak on their behalf they had to keep quiet. Not only do fighting intellectuals act on behalf of the disadvantaged and so prevent them from acting on their own behalf, they also ensure that the disadvantaged have nothing to say. If the disadvantaged, whoever they may be, do speak up, their ability to make themselves heard proves to the fighting intellectuals that they are not disadvantaged. On the other hand, if rich fighting liberal intellectuals want to spend their own patrimony on those whom they consider disadvantaged, let them do so. No one can quarrel for long with people undertaking what they think are good works. No one is likely to raise major objections if they receive tax deductions for their trouble. After all, charity is no bad thing. But does the earnest pursuit of their own particularist moral vision justify them in imposing it on everyone else? And is compulsory charity exacted through taxes still charity? If not, what is its moral weight? One is inevitably reminded of the "vanguard theory" of another fighting intellectual, Lenin. Let us see why.

Trudeau has said of himself that he would accept no discipline other than self-discipline; it was, he said, "unacceptable that others should claim to know better than I what was good for me." And yet, because he always knew he had to speak for the voiceless and act on behalf of the disadvantaged, he would cheerfully use the state to discipline others. There is yet another paradox or deception at the heart of Trudeau's vanguard doctrine. The disadvantaged, however defined, are characterized chiefly by being or being said to be incapable of taking responsibility for themselves. Because of their disadvantages, which prevent them from competing on an equal basis, they are excused from the exercise of their rights. The consequence is that they have no individual responsibilities: once disadvantaged, always disadvantaged. If the disadvantaged lack the capacity for individual responsibility, there is no need for fighting intellectuals to treat them as individuals. Instead, they are simply, "the disadvantaged," and it is the fighting intellectuals who discover their interests and translate their discoveries into public policy, as in "the role of the federal government is to distribute wealth from the affluent to the disadvantaged."

In short, Trudeau takes pride in ensuring that those whom he wishes to benefit can never take pride in themselves. By feeling pride in his own accomplishments on their behalf, the liberal fighting intellectual even denies them the democratic right of determining and speaking up for their own interests. That is, the first act of the liberal fighting intellectual is to appropriate the voices of those whom he or she wishes to help. Thus the question of whether or not these alleged beneficiaries ever were truly voiceless need never arise. As we shall see, Trudeau's initiative in the area of "participatory democracy" raised mere bad faith to a higher power: its practitioners could feel good about helping those who never asked for help and who, by being "helped," were made dependent on the "caregivers." This was truly the higher mendacity.

To understand how the paradox of the fighting intellectual was expressed in the political actions of Trudeau and the gang, we must bear in mind that he was, after all, a Quebec intellectual and Quebec was a comparatively small pond. Even so, the centre of Trudeau's political attention always was, and still remains, Quebec. He grew up under the political regime of Maurice Duplessis and the social tutelage of the Roman Catholic church. His experiences beyond the borders of Quebec, first as a member of a family that travelled in style and then as a young man with a backpack and a shoestring budget, taught him just how backward and obscurantist Quebec was in the 1940s and 1950s, especially its intellectual life. He became a leftist agitator, sure in his opinions and burning with the fervour of moral truth.

In 1960, at age forty-one, he finally landed an acceptable day job, teaching constitutional law. Five years later he decamped for Ottawa, concerned, as he said in his *Memoirs*, about "national unity and the place of Quebec within Canada." But as a man of the left, he was also convinced that the growing separatist movement was "reactionary." The meaning of "reactionary" in this context is not clear, so we must digress briefly.

During the 1960s Quebec nationalists adopted the rhetoric of the far left and spoke easily of the colonization of Quebec by an imaginary entity called "English Canada," which evidently included many citizens of the United States. Calls by self-styled revolutionary leaders to commence the national liberation of the Quebec people were reminiscent of the rhetoric of Fidel Castro, whom Trudeau professed to admire. Pierre Vallières's *White Niggers of America* claimed that the position of French Quebeckers in Canada resembled that of the Afro-American descendants of slaves in the United States. By the mid-1960s the assimilation of Quebec nationalism to Third World liberation fantasies was well under way.

Most people comparing the language of a Quebec nationalist to that of such prominent Communist revolutionary leaders as Castro or Ho Chi Minh might easily conclude that the Quebec nationalists were, in fact, leftists. But according to Trudeau they were reactionary. In the common jargon of the left, to be a reactionary was to be on the right.

So: what is going on here? In what sense were the Quebec nationalists, with their pretensions to national liberation and so forth, "reactionary"? The answer, it seems to us, requires an understanding of the limitations of ideological (as distinct from common-sense) thinking.

Let us take a well-known example from the 1930s, the opposition between the National Socialists of Germany and the International Socialists of the Soviet Union. For many years, the Nazis were disparaged as reactionary and the Communists were praised as progressive, and even today, among some intellectuals, they still are. (Of course, such intellectuals admit, Stalin was responsible for certain deeply regrettable excesses.) One who was not already committed to the doctrine of progress, however, would see the quarrel of Nazis and Communists as strictly intramural: two kinds of socialists disputing the proper way to achieve their unachievable dream. With the doomed Mercutio one would say, "A plague o' both your houses!"

Trudeau's remarks about the Quebec nationalists are a toned-down version of the disputes between national and international socialists. In *Federalism and the French Canadians*, for example, he could despise with great wit the nationalists' sectarian devotion to "the Holy Nation."

> The separatist devout and all the other zealots in the Temple of the Nation already point their fingers at the non-worshipper. And a good many non-believers find it to their advantage to receive their nationalist sacrament, for they hope thus to attain sacerdotal and episcopal, if not pontifical, office, and to be permitted thereby to recite prayers, to circulate directives and encyclicals, to define dogma, and to pronounce excommunication, with the assurance of infallibility. Those who do not attain the priesthood can hope to become churchwardens in return for services rendered; at the very least they will not be bothered when nationalism becomes the state religion.

In response, Daniel Latouche, sometime aide to Lévesque, has shown that anti-separatism, including that of Trudeau, is also a kind of messianic political movement. Perhaps there is something in the waters of the St. Lawrence as it passes between Lachine and Dufferin Terrace that accounts for these fine splenetics. Perhaps Trudeau and Latouche are both right; if so, illumination can come from neither. We cannot progress very far along the path of understanding by trying to make analytical sense of one set of fantastic ideological remarks directed at opposed and equally fantastic ideological positions.

In the case of Trudeau, he might be characterized as a communitarian who rejected the attempt to draw the borders around the community of Quebec and preferred the larger community of Canada, suitably transformed so as to be more to his liking. For him, Quebec was too small a pond. Trudeau was clearly ambitious; it is less clear whether he was principled.

In the case of the nationalists, it has always been clear that they were not principled. As Lord Durham pointed out, the leaders of the Rebellion of 1837 in Lower Canada were essentially modern and liberal politicians out to promote their own interests by awakening genuine anti-liberal sentiments among the credulous and backward *habitants*, and since then any attempt to disguise those interests as transcendent moral, communal, or political principles has been something of a joke, not to say a tasteless failure. That is why, for example, the current crop of nationalists have so easily abandoned the Third World rhetoric of a few years ago. They never really believed it anyway. To borrow Stephen Schecter's phrase, they were already postmodern: if today they are still nationalists keen on independence, the reason is not because they find independence attractive for one reason or another — for instance, because it holds out the promise of justice, to say nothing of national liberation — but because it can be done. "Independence for Quebec is a fine thing," say the present-day nationalists, "because we have the will to achieve it." Like Papineau in 1837, they are pleased to invoke their symbols: both the old symbols in which they no longer believe but that nevertheless serve to express their own resentment — the fate of the Acadians, the Conquest, Louis Riel (of all people!); and the new — the failure of Meech, the hidden agenda of the Reform Party, and so on.

The mutual recriminations of Trudeau and the nationalists, then, are the perfect contextual expressions of *mauvaise foi*. Though lively and entertaining, they are little more than symptoms of a problem that in *Deconfederation* we called "the Quebec Question." And symptoms should never be mistaken for diagnosis or analysis, let alone treatment.

Before considering some of the policy achievements of the Trudeau years, it may be useful to bring together the themes we have been developing. When Trudeau won the leadership of the Liberal party, the outgoing prime minister, Lester Pearson, observed that many of his senior cabinet colleagues were bewildered by his victory. "How," asked Paul Martin, Sr., "can someone who knows nothing of politics or the party get so much support so suddenly, even from people like Joe Smallwood?" Trudeau had no experience and Joey, the Only Living Father of Confederation, had lots of it; so what happened? Pearson's interpretation is not particularly flattering to his own party: according to him, all the other candidates were too closely identified with Mackenzie King. It is as good an interpretation as any, and shows that an old warhorse like Martin was aware that something portentous had taken place.

In our view, Trudeau was indeed a portent. Governments in Canada had been thoroughly corrupted by the Diefenbaker/Pearson agenda: by the late 1960s Canadians had learned to expect "vision" from their leaders, not good government, moderate politics, or sensible policies. Trudeau rejoiced in his intellectual cleverness; in defeat and in retirement he still considered his "ideas" a badge of honour. But those who understand politics in terms of "ideas" tend to be blind to the real sources of their opinions — their own real-life experiences. And Trudeau, as Martin said, had no political experience. But Trudeau was ambitious, and he had plenty of ideas and the energy to put them into action. In April

1968, he was at last in a position to do so.

In *Federalism and the French Canadians* he had written: "We must separate once and for all the concepts of state and nation and *make* Canada a *truly* pluralistic and polyethnic society." Anyone who proposes seriously to *make* a regime *truly* something or other has announced a program of political action that is bound to create havoc. The great revolutionaries are familiar with the language of making rather than persuasion in the realm of politics. Was it not Lenin who drew the obvious analogy from the cook's wisdom: just as you can't make an omelette without breaking eggs, neither can you make a country truly as you will it to be without breaking heads? Excepting only the founders of the American republic, the great modern revolutionaries have left the world worse, by any standard one cares to invoke, than it was when they found it. This gives us a pretty clear indication of the response we would make to Trudeau's own self-proclaimed test for his administration: "Was Canada a better place in 1984 than in 1968?" Decidedly not.

In keeping with the imagery of fabrication, Trudeau wanted to "make" two things when he took office in 1968. First, he would make Canada the kind of place where Quebeckers would feel at home anywhere. And second, he would make Canada, including the now comfortable and well-adjusted Quebeckers, a just society. His tool would be the state.

The first bit of remaking Trudeau had to do concerned what he, along with so many other French Quebeckers, called English Canadians. These people, he said, "will have to retire gracefully to their proper place, consenting to modifying their own precious image of what Canada ought to be." One cannot help noticing that the language of making Canada into something it is not (yet) takes a distinctly aggressive tone when the focus is on Trudeau's will. If "English Canadians" did not retire gracefully, it was clear that

Trudeau would gracelessly put them in their proper place. Trudeau did not provide many details about what the proper place of "English Canadians" was, but it involved atoning for the fact that the French of Quebec did not feel at home elsewhere in Canada. For most Canadians, however, and for sensible people elsewhere, politics is not a kind of public therapy. If the French of Quebec do not feel at home beyond the borders of that province, why should "English Canadians" care one way or another? Because, Trudeau explained in *Federalism and the French Canadians*, "French and English are equal in Canada because each of these linguistic groups has the power to break the country. And this power cannot yet be claimed by the Iroquois, the Eskimos, or the Ukrainians." If, however, the Iroquois or the Ukrainians were in a position to "break" the country, matters would presumably be different. Trudeau apparently subscribed to the view that separatism was a sufficiently grave threat that the demands of the French of Quebec must be granted, whether these demands made sense or not. That is, Trudeau, like so many other federalists mesmerized by the Quebec question, never stopped to wonder whether it was *possible* to grant the things demanded by Quebec. If someone is bound and determined not to feel at home, nothing you can do will ever make them feel differently.

Let us examine the logic of Trudeau's argument: the chief complaint of the French of Quebec was that they did not feel at home outside Quebec; the chief reason for that complaint was that the "English Canadians" were out of place, because their precious image of what the country ought to be was somehow faulty. For all we know, the Iroquois, the Inuit, and the Ukrainians may also not feel at home and for the same reasons. Certainly the Mohawks don't seem to feel at home in Quebec. When it was not in their power to break the country, we could ignore them. But now that they are in a position, if not to break the country, then to break criminal laws against smuggling, we must take them seriously. Law, it seems, is no more than the will of the strongest — and in some circumstances the Government of Canada looks anything but strong when compared, say, to the Mohawks.

It is not clear whether Trudeau was being cynically realistic or was simply whining, blaming others — the "English" — for perfectly understandable problems. Moreover, on occasion, as in his article, "Some Obstacles to Democracy in Quebec," Trudeau could be lucid and insightful. But what did he think should be done? For Trudeau, the answer was as clear and distinct as a Cartesian idea: we make the country in a different image, the image of true pluralism. Moreover, the means were at hand: act on the recommendations of Pearson's B & B Commission and make Canada officially bilingual. Thus was born the Official Languages Act of 1969. Trudeau later called resistance to his new vision "cultural racism" and evoked the insufferably parochial example of a local Montreal hockey team to indicate what biculturalism meant.

During the 1968 election campaign, Trudeau often used a phrase coined by F.R. Scott to express how he saw his refashioned Canada: the "Just Society." In his view, social justice was intimately tied to bilingualism. It is for this reason that he put his old friend Gérard Pelletier in charge of an array of programs at the office of the Secretary of State (SOS) that were designed to secure both participatory democracy and the Just Society. Under Pearson, SOS had provided shock troops for the battles for national unity; in 1969 it received responsibility for the official languages program. There is no doubt, as Les Pal showed in *Interests of State*, a brilliant dissection of SOS, that the initiatives for changing the traditional relation between the state and society, always before based on liberal principles upholding the independence of the voluntary sector, were taken in response to changes in Quebec.

For example, a new administrative branch, Social Action, was created in 1969 within the office of the Secretary of State. According to the 1970 annual report, the Social Action Branch was in charge of "a program which, by utilizing the services of professionally trained community development officers, attempted an in-depth attack on mass apathy and concentrated, during the past months, on sensitizing and preparing confirmed or potential leaders through group dynamic sessions and leadership training courses." All the buzzwords were there: "professionally trained community development officers," not amateur and certainly not untrained persons enlisted from communities; an "in-depth attack on mass apathy" that the allegedly apathetic but perhaps content and certainly not harmful "masses" had never asked for — who, indeed would ask to be attacked? And of course the attack took the form of "sensitizing" and then recruiting (called "preparing") confirmed or potential leaders by means of "group dynamic sessions," whatever they may be, and "leadership training courses." In this way, like frogs' legs in high school experiments, the apathetic masses would be galvanized into twitching, dynamic leaders. In fact, it was rather like another sixties silliness, "organizing a spontaneous demonstration." Social Action assumed what it set out to prove, that there was a pressing need for "better understanding between the two official linguistic communities," and that this need would be met either through "consolidating" things where they were okay and, where they were not, "bringing about a change in attitude among the majority." The majority may be forgiven for having misconstrued the activities of the Social Action Branch as an attempt to shove French down their throats.

One of the programs within the Social Action Branch, namely the Social Animation Program, was directed not at the apathy of the majority but at that of the minority: "Social animation of a minority will encourage its development and enable it to combat the major causes of cultural assimilation, apathy and indifference." The first step in such a program was to train "animators," who, in turn, would provide the hands-on stimulation. In other words, SOS would wander the highways and byways of the country in search of minority language communities, many of them happily assimilating to the larger language community, in order to "animate" them out of their apathy and into dynamic resentments. A close reader of Lenin would have no difficulty in descrying the outlines of his famous program of "agitation and propaganda" in SOS.

From defending the brave new mandate of official bilingualism, it was a short step to the animation of other sectors of society. In 1970, Bernard Ostry was made assistant under-secretary for citizenship and told by Trudeau to shake up the Citizenship Branch and use it to promote "national unity." What he did, according to journalist Sandra Gwyn, writing in *Saturday Night*, was to turn Citizenship "into a flamboyant, free-spending *animateur sociale*. Traditional, father-knows-best groups were upstaged. Instead, massive grants went out to militant native groups, tenants' associations and other putative aliens of the 1970s." The oddity in the Trudeau-Pelletier initiative in the area of "social animation" is that they thought that all this activity and dynamics would promote national unity. If Trudeau and Pelletier had had any political experience or permitted even a modest injection of common sense into the stream of their ideas they might have concluded that stirring up otherwise tranquil citizens in the name of overcoming their apathy might produce the opposite of unity. But intellectuals practising the politics of making never doubt that they will succeed. That, after all, is what good ideas are for.

And yet, things did not work out. As Pal pointed out, more in sorrow than in anger, "it is sometimes said that Canada lives in a perpetual identity crisis. Federal policy since 1970 institutionalized that crisis. Thus the SOS's funding of groups fragments rather than unifies national identity. This is, of course, ironical and perhaps even a bit perverse." For the intellectuals at the helm of the ship of state, since everything should have worked out, it was simply unintelligible when it did not. That is why, for example, *Towards a Just Society* is such a fascinating document: looking back on the mess they created, the Trudeau gang cannot avoid admitting that things went terribly wrong; but they think the reason why it went wrong is that they did not go far enough. Here we touch again on the higher reaches of mendacity where intellectuals wilfully part company with political reality. In the language of contemporary psychobabble, these people are deeply into denial. They sense it, too, even if they don't really know it or admit it.

Other perversities emerged in the wake of Trudeau's 1968 victory. His own summary of the campaign was: "Yes to anything that would make us more free and more equal." Liberals, particularly liberals who are often called conservatives, have often drawn attention to the fact that more freedom and more equality are often antithetical. More freedom can easily lead to less equality as the strong, the clever, or the vicious are at liberty to triumph over the weak, the stupid, and the nice. Does anyone really believe that weak, stupid, nice guys will ever finish anywhere but last? On the other hand, as we saw in chapter 1, greater equality can be attained only by suppressing or regulating or in one way or another interfering with the liberty of individuals to do as they please. As we also saw in chapter 1, there is a big difference between a government that secures equal rights for citizens and one that assures equal results.

In order to reconcile the tension between liberty and equality and design policies intended to secure "economic rights," it was necessary to add the third member of the French Revolutionary slogan, fraternity. In Canada, of course, we prefer the gender-neutral term "national unity." From this perspective, derived from Rousseau not Locke, government coercion is unnecessary: all that is needed is better communication. In the language favoured by SOS, a little "social animation" will produce "better understanding" because there really are no conflicting interests and so "national unity" becomes an intelligible policy objective. The unhappy reality is that Rousseau was wrong. Communitarians never figure this out until after the damage has been done; sometimes even then, as we know, they prefer to blame others rather than rethink their own views.

In any event, Trudeau pushed along his program for the Just Society. "Our first task," Trudeau said, "was to fund and consolidate the great reforms in social welfare inaugurated by the Pearson government." The catalogue of "reforms" is well known. Trudeau's Liberals would help the old by indexing Old Age Security pensions and help the young by using the state to create Opportunities for Youth. One would have thought that any "youth" who had to have an opportunity created for him or her by the government would be unlikely to have sufficient ambition or energy to take advantage of it — unless, as so many did, they were seeking a career in government itself. For those who were too old to be youths but too young to start collecting old age pensions, there were the reforms to the Unemployment Insurance scheme to fall back on.

In 1971, for example, changes to the Unemployment Insurance Act raised payments from 40 per cent of insured earnings to two-thirds. New categories of beneficiaries were created; the qualifying period was shortened and the benefit period extended. In short, whatever resemblance Unemployment Insurance ever had to insurance, which, as we saw, was little enough in any case, was gone. The new structure opened up vast areas for potential abuse for those with sufficient imagination and inclination. It discriminated in favour of areas of high unemployment and against those who were productive, namely employed persons in high employment areas. In short, the reforms of 1971 turned the UI scheme into yet another underhanded means of income transfer from the productive to the unproductive. For those who contributed for years without ever drawing benefits it was simply another tax for which they received nothing in return. And, of course, when the rate of unemployment increased, costs did as well, with a corresponding decline in revenue. Seasonal workers with high earnings, such as fishermen, could earn a very decent wage and then collect pogey until the following season. For the working poor, as distinct from the working middle class, generous UI benefits are a clear and strong disincentive to work.

For the Trudeau gang, however, it was not enough that their social policy constituted an underhanded means of redistributing income, provided the basis for what Yair Aharoni called the No-Risk Society, and attempted to make a world where there were no losers. They forgot, or perhaps they never knew, that there then would be no winners either — except themselves and those who administered their programs. For example, Jimmy Coutts, in his contribution to *Towards a Just Society*, said that social policy ought to be more than social security. It should be concerned with quality-of-life issues. Here the objective was to join social welfare and participatory democracy so that those who "needed" help should also help design it. This, Coutts said, would give them dignity as well as cash, as if dignity were a kind of bonus that made the cash smell good.

Coutts also discovered that all programs could be seen to inter-connect: a "fair" language policy was needed so as to ensure "fair" access to work. A "fair" regional equalization was needed so that a better life, which is to say, a more prosperous life, would be "fair-ly" distributed across the country. Otherwise people without the required language skills or people living where there was nothing to do could not "share" in Canada's bounty. This was especially true, Coutts said, for young Canadians who had no skills, no ini-tiative, no intelligence, no ambition. Such persons, he seriously maintained, were the future of the nation and if their future was bleak, national salvation would come from helping them. And if they drifted aimlessly into drugs, booze, and UI abuse, they had to be helped even more urgently.

The wonder of it is, no one ever asked *why* they had to be helped. The notion that druggies and UI cheats could be held responsible for their own actions and punished never seemed to have crossed the mind of any important Liberals. Instead of responsibility, what was needed were more programs to help these unfortunate, misunderstood brats adjust. Such was the origin of the Opportunities for Youth Program, which Pearson had shelved and which Ostry and Trudeau now revived. Likewise a Local Ini-tiatives Program was dreamed up to help the "disadvantaged" and give them a new lease on life, dignity, happiness, and a sense of peace with all the world. Even better, it would help Native people, too, and who could be more "disadvantaged" than they? The answer to that depended on whom you asked. Some evidently successful women certainly said they *felt* disadvantaged, notwith-standing their successes, much as some French Quebeckers felt unwelcome outside their home province, and that was enough to compare them usefully with the disabled, who undoubtedly *were* disadvantaged. After all, it may be an even greater disadvantage to feel that way and not look disadvantaged to others. This is the hidden disadvantage of low self-esteem. What was needed, clearly, were more social animators to ensure *not* that whiners with low self-esteem grew up or shut up, but that the rest of us became more sensitive to their problems. In the event, task forces were formed and new cabinet responsibilities created and more and more groups who apparently could not help themselves lined up to be helped.

Medicare was the jewel in the social welfare crown. For intellectuals who fret about such things, it was said to be part of our national identity and a major component in the way we distinguish ourselves from the Americans. (One can always tell Canadians sitting in a Paris café or a Bavarian beer garden: they are the ones bragging about medicare, eh?) According to Coutts, in the early 1980s Canada was in danger of developing a two-tiered medical care system — one for the rich and one for the poor. In the mid-1990s Canada has a fully developed two-tiered medical care system. The difference is that in 1980 both tiers were in Canada. Now the upper tier is in the United States. Anyone who can afford the best medical care, such as Quebec's former premier, Robert Bourassa, cross-border shops.

Trudeau, like most intellectuals, claimed to be a man of reason. In place of what he considered to be the unfocused decision making of the Pearson era, Trudeau would inject reason and expertise; the panoply of social science technology would be coupled to that great desideratum "participatory democracy." This was surely a peculiar vision, since administrative efficiency, which is one manifestation of reason, does not get on well with widespread participation in decision making. Unless, that is, one adds to the equation a heady dose of imaginary Rousseauist cooperative goodness. In any event, Trudeau pressed on. He spent his summer holidays after the 1968 election, he said, "putting in place a more rational (my obsession!), better organized system" in the Privy Council Office. The result, according to him, was that cabinet ministers had to know about each other's responsibilities. "It allowed us," he said, "to address the major questions of the day in a rational manner, and it vastly improved the quality of the decisions taken by government." Observers less close to events were able to detect something else.

Nicole Morgan cited Trudeau's close friendship with Michael Pitfield, who became his clerk of the Privy Council, as an important element in dissolving the barrier between bureaucracy and politics. The Trudeau-Pitfield reforms and models of rationalization, she said, "paid little or no attention to experience, expenditures and administrative life as it really exists." The consequence was that, when things refused to work out right, they could blame the model and construct another one. The Trudeau-Pitfield reforms had two tentacles. First, planning the future. What used to be an enterprise confined to astrologers and Soviet Five-Year Charades, was given a new incarnation with Robert McNamara's "reform" of the Pentagon and statistical prosecution of the Vietnam War. Michael Kirby, a mathematician by training, brought the McNamara approach to Ottawa in the guise of systems analysis. It proved as reliable an index of sound policy as McNamara's "body counts" did of American military triumphs. The second tentacle was the "obsession" mentioned earlier by Trudeau. When cabinet became a "coordinating" mechanism, ministers were effectively prevented from ever running their own departments. Since everything had an impact on everything else, all decisions had to be "coordinated" through the labyrinthine civil service that was itself "coordinated" by the PCO.

This "rational reform" had so great an impact on the bureaucracy that the country has not yet recovered. For a start, a new breed of official, the "superbureaucrat," was created. For these men and, increasingly, women, the old barriers to advancement, the need for seniority and experience, were gone. Competition for, and winning of, dollars and programs and person-years (PYs) had their own fascination. So programs expanded, as we have seen; and this meant that central interdepartmental "coordination" expanded as well. The PCO spawned the Federal-Provincial Relations Office, the Ministry of State for Social Development, and the Ministry of State for Economic and Regional Development. Old-style line departments had to respond to all this "coordination" with new planning divisions charged with the production of their own prophetic documents that, in turn, would have to be coordinated by prophets higher up using computers and similar sophisticated devices. All this activity entailed a vast expansion of the civil service: between 1969 and 1976 it increased in size by 37 per cent.

In the early 1970s Ottawa simply went on an administrative binge. And as with the binge of a drunkard, the smallest cost was the price of booze. The drunkard's family paid the real cost. First, there was great instability as hordes of new public servants were on the move ever upward. Some of these whiz-kids moved up so rapidly no one could ever judge the quality of their performance. Any time there is an increase in promotions and transfers, any opportunity to acquire experience and familiarity along with responsibility is lost. Second, the need for lots of officials to "control and coordinate" meant that headquarters staff grew much more than did the field offices. The view then developed that life in the provinces actually delivering whatever service existed was exile. The action was all in Ottawa, which was increasingly filled with colonels, generals, and field marshals, rather than privates, corporals, and sergeants. By 1975, Morgan said, the public service was "hooked on growth as if it were a drug." Inflation increased and any attempt at economic restraint, let alone management, was abandoned.

Trudeau's and Kirby's understanding of reason as organization, rather than as insight based on common sense, led to great emphasis on what we now call "the process." In fact, "the process" is directionless wheel-spinning. Too much "coordination" meant a lot of unread cabinet documents, which meant that cabinet ministers didn't bother to attend meetings for which they were unprepared and where they were likely to be bored. But deputy ministers did attend, and the line between public policy and public administration grew increasingly notional. When ministers had to "coordinate" with their colleagues and no longer really ran their own departments, they no longer saw themselves as responsible or accountable: the system had relieved them of the burden of politics. By the same token, the prime minister and the PMO took up the slack. Cabinet ministers took their cues from an increasingly powerful prime minister (or from his unelected aides) and the more assertive ministers were replaced by quieter diplomatic types who seemed to be content with the endless process of interdepartmental coordination.

"Reason," along with his experience of politics under Duplessis and his evident *ressentiment* at the precious image of Canada held by "English Canadians" lay behind Trudeau's most famous initiative, to establish a constitutionally entrenched bill of rights to protect citizens against both provincial and federal governments. Two questions may be raised on this account: first, could any prime minister get a charter to which the provinces would agree without at the same time engaging in a general constitutional overhaul? In 1965 Trudeau had written, correctly in our view, that opening the constitutional can of worms was irresponsible. Yet he opened it.

Second, it is questionable whether a constitutionally entrenched bill of rights was needed. Two of the foremost constitutional authorities of the day, Peter Russell and Don Smiley, had grave reservations on this score and in both cases their arguments were prudential. "For," Smiley wrote in his presidential address to the Canadian Political Science Association, "in the nature of things there is no sure and certain way to protect human rights — no certainty that courts will be more zealous than legislatures in meeting the future requirements of human freedom and dignity and no certainty, but rather the reverse, that a judiciary intent on defending such rights will long be able to restrain a community bent on their destruction." The point to be made with respect to the Charter of Rights and Freedoms that grew out of this early initiative is concerned less with the reality of civil or human rights, for both Smiley and Russell and others who have become known as "Charter sceptics" are strong advocates of civil and human rights; rather it is that Trudeau's strong advocacy of constitutional entrenchment was a consequence of his even stronger advocacy of "reason" in politics.

In any case, Trudeau's understanding of the Charter was as internally inconsistent as the document itself has turned out to be. On the one hand, he observed in *Towards a Just Society*, "only the individual is the possessor of rights," an opinion with which every liberal might agree. "The spirit and substance of the *Charter* is to protect the individual against tyranny," he said. But in the same sentence Trudeau opened the door to the collectivist doctrine of group rights: "not only that of the state but also any other [tyranny] to which the individual may be subjected by virtue of his [or her] belonging to a minority group." In the first place, it is surely simply an error to apply the term tyranny to anything other than the state. Prejudice, social ostracism, bad attitudes, and nasty looks are not examples of tyranny, however regrettable they may be in other respects. Anti-discrimination laws are clearly within the ambit of liberal constitutionalism, but group rights to equal outcomes seems an unwise or imprudent, because impossible, policy to attempt to constitutionalize. That, too, is part of the Trudeau legacy.

The 1972 election was fought on the empty slogan "The Land Is Strong" and ended with the Liberals in control of a minority government dependent on the NDP for support. Trudeau apparently found the result satisfactory: "I was thus able to institute policies that I had been dreaming about for a long time, and the social-democratic faction of the Opposition [i.e., the NDP] was forced to support them, or else deny their own social program." Domestically, Trudeau's alliance with the socialists entailed an even more generous welfare policy, on the one hand, and the start of serious planning, which was called "industrial strategy," on the other. The compound result was called by Mitchell Sharp the "Third Option."

What made the "Option" the third one was the rejection of the first two: to maintain the status quo or to seek opportunities for free trade with the United States. In fact, these two "options" were one, since the status quo was not static but was beginning to offer opportunities to Canadian companies to enter the U.S. market. The Third Option was the option of Fortress Canada, one of the most ill-considered pieces of nationalist resentment in Canadian history.

The Third Option, suitably, had three components: (1) protectionism, which was justified as an attempt to strengthen Canadian ownership; (2) diversification of Canadian external trade; (3) protection of "Canadian culture." All three components, which taken singly had a certain plausibility to them, had in common one thing: increased intervention by the state in the operation of the economy and in the daily lives of ordinary citizens.

In his contribution to *Towards a Just Society*, Joel Bell confessed that most of the Trudeau cabinet were activists and interventionists, but "in retrospect, it is apparent that the ingredients for an active plan were missing." Bell did not indicate directly what was needed, though he did allow that business leaders "did not perceive or share the government's vision of risk-sharing joint efforts that would, through shared financial involvement, presumably be market-tested pursuits of commonly identified projects and priorities." There were good reasons why business did not share such a cock-eyed "vision." Bell's "presumably" is transparent sophistry. If the pursuits were market-tested there would be neither need nor opportunity for government "sharing." The only time governments "share" in risk or in capital is not when market tests are run but when the market has tested a product and the product has failed the test. Then the government finds overriding reasons to intervene in the market and, inevitably, to make things worse. In this way it bails out companies that otherwise would go bankrupt.

In foreign affairs, Trudeau's policy, in his own eyes, was an example of "liberal idealism at work in a conservative age." In the perceived trade-off between guns and butter, there was no doubt where Liberal priorities lay. As a result, as J.L. Granatstein and Robert Bothwell said at the end of their survey of Trudeau's foreign policy, he was nothing more than "an adventurer in ideas, with great articulation and little commitment." Fighting intellectuals make a hash of foreign policy too.

The end of the second Trudeau government was suitably sordid. After following the "dreams" of the NDP for a couple of years, Trudeau, Allan MacEachen, and John Turner put together a budget they knew would be defeated. The NDP could not stomach one part of it and the Tories would find another part equally rebarbative. But the public opinion polls looked good: "If it's called manipulative," Trudeau mused, "then so be it.... If this kind of maneuvering breeds cynicism about politics," he wrote, "it shouldn't." At least one should not be surprised when self-conscious manipulators appear comfortable with a cynical electorate. Canadians, in fact, believed they had elected a government to conduct the nation's business, not a clique determined to perpetuate itself in office by calling an election two years into the life of Parliament simply because the polling numbers were favourable.

Following the 1974 election, which resulted in a Liberal majority, Trudeau took "six months or so to develop a thoughtful program and timetable for the next four years." Central to his program was the importance of "fairness." Prior to his time at Harvard, Trudeau was of the view that, "business was there to produce the goods and services, and the state was there to provide the proper environment for the production of wealth." But Harvard taught him differently: "the state has an active role to play in ensuring that there is equilibrium between the constituent parts of the economy, the consumers and the producers." Accordingly, when he viewed Thatcherism, Reaganism, and what in his *Memoirs* he called "Mulroneyism," and even when he viewed their derivatives in Eastern Europe, "I just felt that this was wrong, wrong, wrong." What made it all so wrong was that neither Thatcher nor Reagan promoted "fairness" as a policy objective. Indeed, they didn't even speak about it. And yet Thatcherism did revive a sick British economy and cure it of what was called the "British disease"; Reaganism produced the longest period of economic expansion in a generation; even Mulroney saw the problem, however poorly he may have tried to act to solve it. The less said about Trudeau's remarks on Eastern Europe the better.

However that may be, "help" from the Ottawa juggernaut continued to pour forth on the heads of Canadians. Visa and Master-Card had been introduced to Canadians only a few years earlier. It was as if the Government of Canada had a brand-new charge card with no spending limit and no monthly minimum to be paid on the outstanding balance. You were going to be "fair" and buy presents for everyone, whether they needed them or not. To keep the cardholders' minds off the need to pay for what they consumed on credit — in plain language, to divert the attention of Canadian taxpayers from the spectre of the inevitable reckoning — Trudeau found an enemy to blame. He chose the one country that has, in fact, been Canada's greatest friend, the one country with which Canadians have more in common than any other, the United States. The "Third Option" was enforced with a vengeance, first with the Foreign Investment Review Agency (FIRA), designed to keep out U.S. investment, then with the promotion of government enterprises, which were an integral part of the "industrial strategy" mentioned above.

Six months before the first victory of the Parti Québécois under René Lévesque in November 1976, Trudeau assured the country that separatism was dead. Lévesque agreed, in his own backhanded way, having become an advocate of "sovereignty-association," the precise meaning of which no one knew. The significance of the Trudeau-Lévesque tournament of champions was clear: Quebec would play good cop/bad cop with Canada. It was, in a way, to be expected. After all, Trudeau had come to Ottawa to promote what was called "French power." He said, in effect, to English-speaking Canada, agree to official bilingualism and all the rest, or the country is gone. The separatists will split Canada in two. But it turned out, with Lévesque, that separatism was never a goal of the PQ after all. What it really sought was sovereignty-association. And whatever that meant, if Quebeckers didn't get it, well, then they would get serious about separation. But, as we pointed out in *Deconfederation*, separatism was always just a threat, not a goal. And as we move into the nineties, nothing has changed. Trudeau, his mind still focused on Quebec, rose to the bait. Nothing like a good fight against all the old enemies to rejuvenate Trudeau's waning energies. At the same time as he dumped money and patronage into Quebec, showing his audience which government had the deeper pockets, which government could do more to "help" Quebeckers, he would introduce more constitutional change.

By the late 1970s the Trudeau Liberals were tired failures. They had tried several forms of economic intervention, all in the name of the public good, and strange new administrative measures, from old-fashioned planning to novelties such as wage and price controls. But nothing worked. "Stagflation" was the new word to describe the results. Interest and unemployment rates were both high. The Quebec question was yet unresolved and westerners were annoyed and irritated at virtually every initiative Trudeau had taken.

For their part, the politicians were greedy, self-serving careerists waxing fat upon perks and untaxed expense accounts; they could look forward to a genteel retirement on indexed and generous pensions or perhaps a brief but lucrative appointment as consul general at a pleasant spot abroad, a posting to UNESCO or the OECD. Civil servants were no better. As Richard Gwyn remarked, long before the Mulroney extravagances, "more and more public servants took advantage of the indexed pensions they had engineered for themselves to retire early. Often, they signed up immediately with their old departments on contract, or, like Simon Reisman, put their contacts and know-how to work as lobbyists, or `consultants' as they preferred to be called." The lesson was learned among junior bureaucrats as well. The real topics of conversation, wrote Harry Bruce, another journalist, were "raises, promotions, transfers, pensions, reclassifications, bureaucratic boondoggles, raw deals, sweet deals, departmental sweatshops, individual rip-offs and the injustices, extravagances, stupidities and blazing absurdities of the effort to make the public service bilingual." So much for the old virtues of public service: frugality and personal integrity. Such was the consequence of removing the line between the Liberal party and the public service. It was indeed aptly symbolized by Trudeau's close personal friendship with Michael Pitfield. In May 1979, the electorate declared it had had enough. Joe Clark, the surprise replacement of Robert Stanfield, led a new, inexperienced and, as it turned out, short-lived and directionless government. In due course, Trudeau resigned and was scheduled to be replaced when the Clark government was defeated.

"Welcome to the eighties," Trudeau proclaimed on February 18 at a Liberal party victory celebration. Welcome indeed! If the election campaign was a sign of what was to come, these would be scoundrel times. After the 1980 victory, Trudeau said he would govern "as though it was going to be my last [term]." That is, he would govern without concern for party responsibility or for the fabric of the country. He was home free, in a position now to care only for his own agenda, his own "ideas." In his version, the issues were four in number: the Quebec referendum, the energy issue, the economy, and the constitution. But, in fact, there were but two issues: Quebec and the constitution were two sides of the same coin, as were energy and the economy. The logic was clear but never could be admitted: if Alberta's energy revenues could be appropriated by Ottawa, and then redirected by it, the economy would hum; if the constitution could be changed, Quebec would be happy to remain in Canada. Even if it proved impossible to change the constitution, the "redirection" of energy revenues as regional equalization payments held the promise of making Bourassa's profitable federalism attractive. But to whom? Surely only to Quebeckers cynical enough to be concerned only with their own short-term interests and devoid of all traces of pride. Even if such people could be persuaded, the difficulties with such a strategy were manifold: first, Ottawa had already shown itself to be the problem, not the solution; second, to attack what was arguably the most dynamic and innovative sector of the Canadian economy, namely the oil and gas industry, was exceptionally stupid even by Ottawa's dimmed lights; third, the logic of separatism-as-threat could best be met, as Trudeau had indicated in 1970, by the War Measures Act, or, under less strenuous circumstances, by hard-nosed politics, but never by appeasement.

The first indication that Canada had fully entered the looking-glass world of the higher mendacity came with the Péquiste-initiated referendum on sovereignty-association. Between May and November 1980, Canadians were treated to a constitutional farce, albeit without the special effects of academic obfuscation that came with the Mulroney years. In those days, the actors were still new to their roles, but they delivered their lines with the purity and conviction that comes from a sincere hope of getting away with something. Lévesque urged Quebeckers to vote "yes" in order "to put our weight on the bargaining table as a people." What would they bargain for? Terms of independence or "better terms," like the old pols from Atlantic Canada during the pre-Confederation period? Once again, the great ambiguity arose — was independence a goal or a threat? Now, at least, we know the answer.

It served Trudeau's purposes to take it as a threat, and he responded with an ambiguous promise of his own: "I can make a most solemn commitment that following a `No' vote we will immediately take action to renew the constitution and we will not stop until we have done that." This was as close as Trudeau came to opening the curtains and exposing his hidden constitutional agenda. He promised renewal but provided no details, which meant he would interpret his own words as he saw fit.

There are many accounts of the nearly two years it took to cut a deal; none of them is particularly edifying. In November 1981 a final agreement was made, but without Quebec. The Quebec delegation whined about having been tricked and betrayed by Trudeau. In fact, Lévesque had been the first to break ranks among the premiers, who had sworn in blood to remain united in opposition to Trudeau. Besides, no self-respecting Quebec separatist could possibly have wished for constitutional renewal. But then again, no advocate of sovereignty-association really wanted independence, either. It was a classic example of *blocage*. When pushed to the wall, Lévesque could only complain: "*Trudeau m'a fourré.*" Politely translated: "We got screwed." Ever since, Quebeckers have been saying the same thing and Canadians are bewildered: "What did we do? We love you! *Mon Canada comprend le Québec!*" and so on. For those few Canadians who could remain spectators, the spectacle of passionate recrimination on the one side and warm-hearted perplexity on the other was the very essence of farce.

On December 2, 1981, the House of Commons sent a request to the British government asking for the constitution to be patriated. That same day flags were flown at half-staff across the province of Quebec. If anything died that day, it was the self-respect of Quebeckers and their faith in the silly, petulant game of bluff, threat, and complaint that successive premiers have so badly played. In the event, the Canada Act, 1982 was passed by the British Parliament and transmogrified into the Constitution Act, 1982 upon becoming proclaimed by Her Majesty, just before it rained in Ottawa on April 17, 1982.

The second, equally mendacious and ill-considered policy that the last Trudeau regime foisted upon the land was the National Energy Program. The context for action by the federal government began with the OPEC-initiated price increases of the early 1970s. In 1972 the Alberta government revised the royalty structure that had been in place since 1948 in order to encourage Canadian-owned junior companies to increase their exploration. In September 1973 Ottawa imposed an export tax on Canadian crude going to Chicago, and in 1974 eliminated the tax provision that allowed oil companies to deduct provincial royalties when calculating income taxable by the federal government. It was a classic example of Ottawa's encroachment on a provincial source of revenue. A similar skirmish took place with respect to natural gas. For many Albertans, the moves by Ottawa looked like another example of federal intrusion on provincial autonomy.

However that may be, there were three elements to the Liberals' 1980 energy platform: (1) they would ensure lower petroleum prices than the Conservatives; (2) they would "Canadianize" the oil industry; (3) they would ensure energy security through self-sufficiency. At the end of the day what the NEP actually achieved was: (1) the highest price increases in Canadian history; (2) a drastic reduction in the importance of the Canadian sector of the oil industry (Dome and Turbo being the chief examples); (3) an increase in supply uncertainty similar to that of the first OPEC crisis because of massive disincentives to conventional exploration in favour of the frontier.

Peter Foster has provided a detailed account of the origins and significance of the NEP. Two of his observations are particularly astute. First, the initiative came from the bureaucrats in the

Department of Energy, Mines and Resources (EMR). The problem, as they saw it, was this: Alberta produced the oil but it was consumed in central Canada. Higher oil prices redistributed wealth through the market to Alberta and, to a lesser extent, to British Columbia and Saskatchewan. This was clearly an "imbalance." As Trudeau said in his *Memoirs*, if the imbalance were left uncorrected, the equalization program would have to be scrapped because "even Ontario would have become a have-not province," which was, of course, totally unthinkable. In short, it was not "fair" that Alberta should collect so much revenue. The ultimate cause of this unfairness was the irrationality of nature in putting oil in Alberta in the first place. Surely it was now up to the rationality of EMR to set things right. More to the point, it was self-evident that Alberta could not be expected to use its new financial power in the interests of Canada. What made it self-evident was the undisputable fact that Albertans had shown their complete irresponsibility, not to say irrationality, by refusing to elect a single Liberal to the House of Commons.

There was, however, another way of looking at the energy problem. If the chief objective of exploration is to find oil, when oil companies had more money they would undertake more exploration. If they found oil, it is true, Alberta would get richer, but Alberta was still widely acknowledged to be part of Canada and had not made any threats, serious or frivolous, to leave. No Albertan had even considered independence as a goal. Whether the pride of Ontario would be shattered if it became a "have-not" province (whatever that meant) and whether or not the regional equalization policy would have to be rethought or even scrapped, the fact is, higher oil prices would ensure greater security of supply.

Foster also drew attention to a second important point, which has been made by many others as well, including Trudeau and his energy minister, Marc Lalonde, namely, that the assumption upon which the whole massive edifice rested — constantly rising oil prices — was wrong. There were to be no shortages of supply and prices were soon to fall. Anyone who had passed Economics 200 could instruct the bureaucrats in Ottawa about markets and such little matters as supply and demand and how these mysterious things are related to prices. High prices for oil during the late 1970s led to lower demand, as conservation measures and product substitution had their inevitable and predictable effects. Lowered demand led to lower prices as companies and producers bid for customers. That is how markets work, including commodity markets. The Ottawa economists and their economically illiterate political masters had forgotten or never learned about the old textbook standby, the corn-hog cycle.

The economic thinking of Trudeau and the gang revealed a great deal about their parochialism, their collectivist commitments, and the imprudence of developing an industrial strategy that aimed at something so artificial and abstract as "fairness." To begin with, Trudeau was of the view that the price of oil was politically determined by OPEC and in no way influenced by the market. If OPEC could operate that way, he reasoned, so could Canada: hence the NEP. Second, foreign oil companies were bad. If they reinvested their profits in Canada, they were bad because they got bigger; if they didn't, they were bad because profits went abroad. By this logic the only good foreign oil companies were those that did not make a profit. But even then they would be bad because they would leave.

Peter Foster reported a revealing conversation between Trudeau and Jack Gallagher, president of the now bankrupt Dome Petroleum, but then one of the chief beneficiaries of the NEP.

Dome had obtained what were called "super-depletion tax allowances," the result of which was that Canadian taxpayers spent a lot of money in Dome's Beaufort Sea exploration play. "Well," said Pierre, "that means they really drilled the hole for free."

"But Pierre," said Jack, "that's not the point. The point is, there is a hole there now and there wasn't before. And at the bottom of that hole is a lot of oil. Besides, the taxes are only deferred, not foregone."

"Well, Jack," said Pierre, "I heard they got it for nothing. That's all." As the oilmen say, Pierre saw the hole, not the doughnut.

A decade after the NEP was extinguished, it still can arouse serious disagreements. The reason, it seems to us, lies in the fact that it exposed the moralizing humbug of the collectivists to the harsh light of economic reality. The NEP was essentially a policy aimed at generating revenue by transferring money from the productive private sector and the productive provinces, especially the three westernmost ones, to Ottawa. The assumption was that state control was preferable to private control where the state meant Ottawa, not Edmonton, and "control" by government was wrongly equated with "control" by private interests. What made the NEP so appealing to some was the claim of the collectivists that it was for the public good. The market and the multinational oil companies are not concerned with the public good. All they are concerned with is creating wealth. The collectivists have a higher purpose — spending wealth for the public good. The credulous will always believe their sweet song of public virtue, and they did. Productive Canadians are still paying for their gullibility.

In the cold light of day, the NEP was an expensive failure and probably the worst of the industrial policies the Liberals invented. But their other attempts at picking winners ahead of time and then laying down taxpayers' money in the hopes of eventual pay-offs were hardly any more successful. They did, however, succeed in keeping failing companies alive and partially insulated from market discipline. To these companies' competitors, this looked a lot like special treatment and special subsidy, which meant that viable companies were soon clamouring for a place at the trough. Regional "equalization," as has been pointed out often enough, played out the same game in terms of geography not industry and had the same perverse consequences.

No government can predict the future. No economist with a trace of honesty can foretell the business cycle. The folk wisdom that we noted in the first chapter, namely that hard times recur and that it is prudent to count on that to happen, carried with it the equally prudent implication that when hard times come you had better cut down on expenses. No one yet has grown prosper-ous by going deeper into debt. Using your credit card to pay tomorrow's bills is a fool's option. It was, however, the option taken by the Government of Canada during the waning years of the Trudeau administration.

The last budget surplus was run in 1972. In every year since then government has run up a deficit. Accordingly, the accumulat-ed debt has risen and governments have grown more constrained in their policy options and more voracious in their appetite for tax revenue. In short, Trudeau's defence of the welfare state, which by 1970 was rapidly becoming obsolete and indefensible, led to mas-sive overspending. The Liberals were grasshoppers on steroids, tak-ing no thought for the morrow and forgetting whatever they once knew about yesterday. They proved themselves to be beyond question the worst custodians of the economy in Canadian history. Their only rivals in the mismanagement sweepstakes would be the Barrett government in British Columbia and the Rae government in Ontario. But those two were both confessed socialist regimes and might at least plead a kind of *déformation professionelle*: no one ever expected a socialist to know about, or care for, the economy. Besides, compared to Trudeau, they did less damage.

Readers who have followed this sorry tale will have noticed that we find much to criticize about the Trudeau watch. It would be wrong to think that he did absolutely nothing worthy of the praise of reasonable persons. There are two areas where, in our view, Trudeau's efforts went initially in the right direction. The first involved his desire to entrench civil and political rights in the constitution. We said earlier that it may not have been prudent to make the attempt because, as Trudeau himself said often enough, opening the constitution for discussion was like opening a can of worms, and it was unlikely in the extreme that the provinces would agree to his project of entrenched rights without a more general constitutional (or megaconstitutional, as Peter Russell called it) discussion. Even so, one can only admire Trudeau's efforts to promote the equality of citizens before the law.

A second area where he deserves the unqualified admiration of liberal and democratic Canadians is in the area of Aboriginal politics. It is known to everyone who cares to look at the question that, as Trudeau said in 1984, "aboriginal peoples have long been victims of severe injustices that are not tolerable in Canadian society." In 1969, early in his political career, Trudeau attempted to change that by turning Native people into Canadians. In a speech in Vancouver given after the White Paper on Indian Policy was released, he said:

> We can go on treating the Indians as having special status. We can go on adding bricks of discrimination around the ghetto in which they live and at the same time perhaps helping them preserve certain cul-

tural traits and certain ancestral rights. Or we can say you're at a crossroads — the time is now to decide whether the Indians will be a race apart in Canada or whether they will be Canadians of full status. And this is a difficult choice. It must be a very agonizing choice to Indian peoples themselves because, on the one hand, they realize that if they come into society as total citizens they will be equal under the law but they risk losing certain of their traditions, certain aspects of a culture and perhaps even certain of their basic rights.

The alternatives, in our view, have changed not a whit since then. Moreover, Trudeau was also right when he said it was "inconceivable that one section of society should have a treaty with another section of a society." Charter or no, citizenship in liberal democracy means equality before a law common to all, not several classes of citizens regulated by several classes of law. That Trudeau was forced to retreat soon after uttering these words was and is, in our opinion, a great misfortune for all Canadians, and especially for Native people.

Nearly all who have written about Trudeau have stressed his personal qualities and the ambivalence of the political results he achieved. What else can one expect when one who spoke so much about nation building left office with the nation he was trying to build in a shambles, weakened economically and infected with a feverish constitutional virus? We would not disagree with these accounts of the mess Trudeau made, for the facts are plain. But we would suggest that one of the reasons he was able to do such damage was precisely because of his much-praised personal qualities: his intelligence, courage, will, and determination.

Don Smiley once said that intellectuals do not always make the best politicians because they filter the world through the intellect. We have Trudeau's admission that he is, or was, "obsessed" with rationality. In *Deconfederation* we poked fun at our university colleagues who mistook themselves for men of affairs. The purpose of professors of history or of political scientists is, in this context, to insist on distinctions. In order to draw up a balance-sheet of the Trudeau years some distinctions must be borne in mind: between theory and practice, "reason" and prudence, the politician and the scholar. One of the reasons, perhaps the chief reason, why Trudeau was able to contribute too mightily to what went wrong is that he combined the otherwise admirable personal qualities indicated earlier (and others besides) with great faith in the power, truth, and virtue of his own ideas. It may be an exaggeration to say that ideas have no place in politics, but it is only a slight and harmless one. We believe, with Senator Norm Atkins, that politics is about friendships, loyalties, and ideas, in that order. Trudeau got the order exactly backwards.

5
The Last Orgy of
Public Virtue

For many months pollsters, pundits and politicians were filled with fears that Canada's 35th Parliament since Confederation would follow the Italian model: no party or even combination of larger parties would have a clear mandate to govern. But early in the evening of October 25, 1993, as the polls began to close across the nation and the results to flash across Canada's television screens, those fears quickly dissipated. A Liberal landslide was in the making; the Progressive Conservative government of Prime Minister Kim Campbell was going down to by far the worst defeat any government has suffered in Canadian history. By the time the evening was over the Tories had been reduced from the 154 seats they held at dissolution on September 8 to just 2 seats, one in Quebec and one in New Brunswick. The Liberals had had their best showing in forty years, winning 178 seats in all and 98 out of 99 in Ontario. The Bloc Québécois captured 54 out of Quebec's 75 seats, while the Reform Party of Canada won 52 seats, mostly in Alberta and British Columbia. What did this event mean?

It is true that Kim Campbell was at the helm when the Tory ship went under, almost without a trace, but the election was more of a national referendum on Brian Mulroney's close to nine years in office than a judgement on Campbell. She had had little time to put her own stamp on government — just 123 days — and had made no concerted effort to distance herself from her predecessor. He, paradoxically, had been the last Tory since John A. Macdonald to win two majority governments in a row but had become one of the most despised men in Canadian political history. Unlike his nearest rival in the unpopularity sweepstakes, Pierre Trudeau, Mulroney seemed to care deeply what people thought of him. It was easy enough to detest Trudeau, but more difficult to hold him in contempt. Mulroney's evident need for approval made it easier for Canadians to sneer when they spoke his name, as if a little bit of personal spite might hurt him where it counted. Apart from his personality, Brian Mulroney was also reviled for his policies. Here the record was mixed, even if popular judgement was not: he was the man who had imposed an unpopular tax (the GST), done nothing to solve unemployment, failed to pay down the debt, and mired the nation in five years of fruitless and painful constitutional wrangling that had led to two spectacular failures — the Meech Lake Accord and the Charlottetown Accord.

Things did not start out that way. On September 4, 1984, Mulroney swept to power with the largest majority in Canadian history, capturing 211 out of 282 seats. He had run against the hapless John Turner. His hungry and ruthless campaign strategists had identified Turner with the Trudeau government's record of patronage, with out-of-control spending, and with an unhappy record of confrontation with the provinces. There were those who suspected that Trudeau had engineered Turner's defeat by demanding and receiving Turner's assurance that he would confirm and extend a final flurry of Trudeau's patronage appointments. From Trudeau's point of view, Mulroney was supremely qualified to continue his own good works: he was, after all, a Quebecker. In the event, of course, Trudeau like so many others, was bound to be disappointed.

Mulroney began his first administration with a solid mandate to initiate fundamental economic change. In accordance with that mandate, Finance Minister Michael Wilson issued a position paper entitled "A New Direction for Canada: An Agenda for Economic Renewal" on November 8, 1984. In it, Wilson summarized the economic position of the nation and laid out options that were intended to form the basis for public consultation about the direction Canada ought to take in the future. The Department of Finance had been working on the paper even before the election. No matter what party won a majority, officials in Finance were certain that the public wanted action and confident that the new government would take action to change the direction Ottawa had been going in since the late 1960s.

The Introduction to the Wilson document reflected this official wisdom: "On September 4, Canadians voted for change.... In doing so, they have provided the opportunity to make a fresh start, to build new confidence and a new national consensus toward achieving the economic promise and potential of Canada. They voted for a change in policies and a change in the approach of government to the making of those policies. That is our mandate and our challenge." There could be no mistake; the Mulroney government understood that its mandate was for economic renewal, not constitutional tinkering.

It might have appeared to some observers that Brian Mulroney was about to return Canada to the path it had left on the defeat of the St. Laurent government almost a quarter of a century before — solid financial management, good government, no messing around with dangerous notions that the federal government had some sort of mission to recast Canada and Canadians in some new, fundamentally different mould, or to define "Canadianism." Tories were supposed to be good financial managers and that was why they had been selected to govern. The Liberals had left the Canadian economy in bad shape. The debt and the deficit were at historic highs and unemployment was higher than at any time since the Great Depression. The Tories would fix all that.

So the Mulroney government set out early to change Canada's economic direction and provide the sort of prudent fiscal management that Canadians craved. How did it do in meeting the desires of Canadians to clean up the economic mess Trudeau had left behind? It is clearly impossible in one chapter to present a full picture and analysis of the economic, fiscal, and monetary policies of the Mulroney government over nine years. Even so, the one conclusion most easily drawn is that the record contains both pluses and minuses:

(1) *Privatization*: Wilson's economic statement opened up the question of whether or not the government's by then vast holding of Crown corporations ought to be reduced: "Although each [Crown] corporation was established to serve what, at the time, might have been an important public policy purpose, we must ask ourselves whether that remains the case. If it does not, it is surely important to consider whether the corporation should be retained." Those were fighting words to Canada's left, which by the 1980s had become traditionalists, genuine economic dinosaurs who still laboured under the illusion that government intervention, and especially government ownership, is the invariable cure

for whatever ails any economy, anywhere in the world at any time in human history. For some reason known only to the left, this inflexible dogma was considered to be particularly apt for Canada. Fortunately for the country, most Canadians strongly disagree.

The Mulroney government moved quickly to establish its *bona fides* in the area of economic common sense. It quickly found a buyer for Toronto-based de Havilland Aircraft (and sold it to Boeing) and Montreal-based Canadair (sold to Bombardier, which then also acquired de Havilland from Boeing). Those two money-losing aircraft manufacturers had been taken over by the Liberals to keep them "alive" and preserve jobs. The Mulroney government also privatized a number of small Crown corporations that few people had ever heard of, and Air Canada, which almost everyone had travelled on at one time or another. There was no move to sell off Via Rail, Canadian National Railways, or the Canadian Broadcasting Corporation, the self-defined icon of Canadian national identity. Petro-Canada was retained as a Crown corporation, although shares were issued to the public. Thus, changes *were* made: a major symbol of Canada's global presence, Air Canada, *was* privatized; Bombardier, surely a shining example of Canadian know-how and entrepreneurship in Quebec, was given a chance to rationalize the Canadian aircraft industry. But other money-losing Crown corporations were left untouched.

(2) *Taxation*: It took great political courage to eliminate the old, hidden, manufacturer's sales tax that put Canadian-made products at a disadvantage compared to similar products from outside Canada's borders. That was because the Canadian products were taxed at source while the foreign products were not and could not be. Also, it was not possible for the government to impose import taxes on most of those foreign-manufactured products because that would invariably have violated trade agreements such as the

General Agreement on Tariffs and Trade (GATT) or, later, the Canada-U.S. Free Trade Agreement (FTA). The answer was to introduce a Goods and Services Tax (GST) at a rate of 7 per cent (with groceries and medications exempted) that would be paid by the consumer at the cash register.

A whole new national bureaucracy was put into place to administer the new GST, which went into effect on January 1, 1991. The government expected to collect substantial new revenues from the GST, particularly since it was believed that people operating in the "underground" economy and not paying taxes would be forced to the surface. In fact, it appears that the opposite has happened; there is clearly widespread non-compliance with the GST, which is probably also leading people to cheat on their income taxes in an effort to hide from the government the fact that they are not collecting the GST from their clients. It is most certainly the case that the government's revenue projections were much higher than the actual amounts collected. Part of this difference may have been a consequence of the serious recession that gripped the national economy at about the time the GST was introduced. But part is clearly also a result of the growth of the underground economy that GST avoidance has stimulated.

One major promise made by Wilson was to follow the example set by the United States under Ronald Reagan to examine the Canadian tax structure with the object of rationalizing it. The study took place and marginal tax rates were lowered. But an examination of the overall taxation picture shows that the nation, in fact, is being taxed much more heavily today than when the Tories took power in 1984. One estimate, by economist Patrick Grady of Ottawa-based Global Economics Ltd., was that the average Canadian family was paying in the neighbourhood of $1,900 more in taxes in 1993 than it was in 1984. The tax increases began with a 5 per cent surtax on income tax in 1985 and have not yet diminished. Another way of considering the Tories' achievement is to look at changes in Tax Freedom Day. This is a measure devised by the Fraser Institute that specifies the day in the year when the average Canadian family has done enough work to pay the tax bill imposed on it by several layers of government. After Tax Freedom Day, the average family starts working for itself; until Tax Freedom Day they are working for Revenue Canada and associated agencies. In 1961 Tax Freedom Day fell on May 3rd; by 1974 it came more than a month later, on June 8th. In 1992 it came on July 7th. In Quebec it came a week later; in Alberta two weeks earlier.

Whatever measure one chooses, the implication is the same: governments evidently find it easier to tackle major economic problems, and especially the deficit, through tax increases rather than through expenditure reduction. The fact that every dollar that flows to Ottawa (or to provincial coffers, for that matter) in taxes is one less dollar to be spent on the purchase of job-producing goods or services was apparently lost on a government that chose not to make hard choices in the matter of social program expenditure.

(3) *Social spending*: The major areas of federal government expenditure in Canada include transfers to the provinces under Established Program Financing (EPF), which includes: payments for programs such as medicare; the Canada Assistance Plan (for a variety of welfare programs); equalization payments; interest on the national debt; defence spending; payments to persons under federally mandated programs such as UI, the Old Age Security (OAS) also known as the old age pension, and the now-defunct family allowance programs; the daily cost of running the government. Of that money paid out by Ottawa which does *not* go to pay interest on the national debt, the federal government in a typical

year will pay approximately 33 cents of every program dollar to individuals, 22 cents to the provinces, 17 cents for the cost of running itself, 11 cents for subsidies to business, agriculture, the research community, etc., 11 cents for defence, 4 cents to underwrite the losses of Crown corporations, and 2 cents for foreign aid (these figures represent 1991 federal budget projections). It is obvious, then, that any serious effort to reduce the deficit has to target transfers to individuals. What, then, was the Mulroney government's record on that score?

In January 1985, Jake Epp, then minister of national health and welfare, issued a "constitutional paper" on Child and Elderly Benefits designed "to assist Canadians to participate in the consultative process on child and elderly benefit programs initiated in the November 8 [1984] economic statement." Just why was the government looking at these benefits? Not for the purposes of spending reductions, that much was certain. In fact, Epp laid out three principles that were supposed to remain inviolate: "universality ... must not and will not be called into question"; means tests were "not appropriate" to determine eligibility for the receipt of child and/or elderly benefits; "any savings which may result from program changes will not be applied to a reduction of the deficit." Thus, as the nation was emerging from the worst recession since the 1930s into what would prove to be a prolonged boom, the government gave notice that it was not interested in reducing the deficit by cutting back on transfers to individuals, even to those individuals who had no actual need of government funds because of their own high income levels. The government claimed it was not even thinking of taxing back benefits from well-to-do Canadians. It was, instead, looking at the child and elderly benefits package to make that package more flexible and "fairer."

Why did the Mulroney government make such rash and

imprudent promises? It did so partly to follow through on an election pledge. For decades Canadians had been told by socially sensitive, not to say socialist, media that Tories were evil-eyed, mean-minded, free enterprisers who could not wait to slash and burn Canada's precious legacy of expensive social programs. For many media types, as we said, Canada's social welfare programs, our famous safety net, were what distinguished us from the Americans, who, though admittedly wealthier than Canadians, were not as nice. What did seem clear, however, is that the anti-Tory animus of the media, at least with respect to their passionate defence of welfare, was based on near-total ignorance of the historical record. The fact that Tory John Diefenbaker had initiated one of the biggest give-aways in social spending in Canadian history to date was conveniently forgotten. But no matter; the media-driven myth made Tory intentions regarding Canada's social programs into one of the major issues of the 1984 election and Brian Mulroney, in that blarney-spinning way of his, rose to the bait. The maintenance of Canada's social programs was a "sacred trust," he told the Canadian public; his government would never trim, eliminate, cut back, or reduce those programs. Thus the government was effectively claiming that it would not touch the more than 40 per cent of its budget that went to individuals. Since it could not touch the more than 20 per cent or so that went to pay interest on the debt, it was declaring that all the deficit reduction it was planning would be carried out only on the remaining 40 per cent or so of the budget — a tall order indeed. Just how Mulroney or Canadian voters thought that any deficit cutting was going to happen was not discussed.

But was the government being honest? There was clearly much confusion among the key ministers, Epp and Wilson, and Prime Minister Mulroney, both about the government's intentions and about what could (or should) be revealed about those intentions. Thus a whole series of mixed signals emanated from Ottawa over the winter and into the early spring of 1985. Then, in May, Wilson gave his first full budget speech and announced that beginning in January 1986, there would be a partial de-indexation of both family allowances and Old Age Security payments; from then on the OAS would be increased only by the amount of inflation less 3 per cent. So, for example, if the rate of inflation was 4 per cent, the increase adjustment would be only 1 per cent. Whether or not this move was justified, wise, or made good economic sense, it clearly was a means of reducing payments to individuals and clearly was a violation of Epp's pledge made just five months earlier.

The partial de-indexing of the OAS was, in fact, intended to be the opening move in a strategy developed by the Department of Finance. The goal was, fully or partially, to de-index income-tax exemptions, family allowances, and the OAS. The government projected that it might save as much as $6 billion by 1991 if it carried through with the program. But it did not. In its first major effort actually to do something about social spending on the way to serious deficit reduction, it ran into public opposition and backed off.

Payments to pensioners in Canada come in two forms; the OAS and the Guaranteed Income Supplement (GIS). The former is a standard amount paid out each month to all eligible pensioners over age sixty-five regardless of any other income they may enjoy. The latter is a special supplement to low-income pensioners determined on the basis of their taxable income. It is important to point out here (especially because it was *not* pointed out by most of the media at the time) that the government was *not* proposing to touch the GIS in any way. Thus low-income pensioners would have continued to receive the GIS and the OAS and, presumably, any decrease they would have had to swallow on the OAS would have been made up by an increase in the GIS.

No matter, there was a hue and cry anyway. The outraged response from senior citizens' groups could have been predicted: their ox had been gored. The reaction of the Canadian Chamber of Commerce and the Business Council on National Issues could not. Both organizations declared that pensions for the elderly should be fully indexed and that the government should find the money for deficit reduction elsewhere. All across the country people organized, signed petitions, and demonstrated; Canadians wanted tough action to put their economic house in order, but only until somebody actually took tough action. Then they became indignant. In June, after a confrontation with angry demonstrators on Parliament Hill, Mulroney forced Wilson to back down. The government retreated from its intention of partially de-indexing the OAS but went ahead in the fall of 1985 with its plan for partially de-indexing family allowances. Many of the same special-interest groups came forward to protest that move, but this time the government held firm and the bill was given third and final reading in January 1986. By then it was too late; the government had allowed itself to become intimidated and took virtually no action on social spending reform for three more years. In 1992, family allowances were eliminated entirely and replaced with supplements for poor families. In effect, the government did what it had rashly promised not to do — eliminate universality as an operating principle and tax back benefits from those who really did not need them. Both moves went in the right direction but were too little, too late. The thoroughgoing review both of special programs and of the complex structure of federal-provincial fiscal relations to which they are directly connected was never carried out.

(4) *Unemployment Insurance*: Although UI payments are, strictly

speaking, part of the social spending envelope, we are treating it here as a separate item because of the impact that UI policy has on unemployment itself. Put simply, Canada has had unemployment rates that have been considerably higher than those of other OECD countries for some time now. At the time of writing, for example, the Canadian rate of unemployment is still over 11 per cent, while the U.S. rate has dropped to about 6.4 per cent of the workforce. Even the rosiest projections do not see the Canadian rate getting into single digit numbers until 1996 at the earliest. When the national Canadian rate is in the 10 per cent range, the rate in large areas of the Atlantic provinces is usually double that.

By virtually any measure, Canada's Unemployment Insurance program is one of the most generous (if not *the* most generous) in the Western industrialized world. Until recently in some parts of Canada, for example, a person need only work ten straight weeks to qualify for forty-two weeks of UI. In 1991 the OECD observed that Canada's UI encourages job seekers to register as unemployed and to prolong their search for work. In addition, the OECD commented, "regionally extended benefits, according to which unemployed persons in high-unemployment provinces are entitled to receive benefits for a longer period ... reduced the incentives for the jobless to search for a job" in another area of the country or sector of the economy. Craig Riddell of the University of British Columbia and David Card of Princeton University have found that Canada spends from four to five times more on UI per capita than the United States (from $15 to $20 billion a year) and that an unemployed Canadian is far more likely to receive UI than an unemployed American. For a long time Canada was one of the few countries where a person who voluntarily quit a job could collect UI.

There is a great deal of independent evidence to show that a generous UI system perpetuates high unemployment in a number of ways. Some of that evidence was placed before a commission of inquiry into the state of UI headed by Claude Forget and appointed by the Mulroney government in 1986. Forget's report basically concluded that UI was no longer insurance in any accepted sense of the word but had become an instrument promoting social assistance and regional subsidization. He recommended a thorough overhaul of the system, including an end to the special regional benefits package. In the face of sustained opposition from regional interests, from Quebec, and from social welfare groups, the government revised most of the commission's proposals.

UI is not, in itself, a major drain on federal finances. The bulk of the funds in the system are contributed by employers and employees. Thus, even if the federal contribution were eliminated entirely, there would be only a small saving in this item of the national budget. But if the experts are right and the system as it exists now is either creating unemployment or allowing high levels of unemployment to persist in Canada as a whole and especially in certain regions of the country, the entire economy suffers. Every person in Canada who is not engaged in gainful employment is a drag on the economy in the form of low purchasing power and a low rate of tax payment. As we mentioned in chapter 3, the real key to Canada's postwar prosperity and its ability to eliminate the deficit was putting people back to work. Canadians need to be put back to work in much larger numbers than we have traditionally been able to do. Our UI system is so generous that it takes roughly 2 per cent of economic growth in Canada to lower the rate of unemployment by 1 per cent. That is unacceptable, and the Mulroney government showed itself too timid to tackle the problem.

(5) *The cost of government*: There can be no question that the Mulroney government's best performance by far in terms of eco-

nomic management was in reducing the cost of running the government. A series of internal reforms carried out from virtually the start of the Mulroney mandate together with wage freezes and a significant downsizing of the public service, mostly through attrition, resulted in real reductions in the daily cost of operations. This, however, is a relatively small budget item.

(6) *Transfer payments to the provinces*: This is the second-largest piece of the program-spending pie. It is also one of the most complex issues that any government has to deal with. In November 1984, Wilson's study paper discussed the need for reform of federal-provincial transfers and proclaimed: "The answer for the future is not simply to top up federal or provincial funding for health and post-secondary education. The answer is not simply more money. We need to talk about ways in which we can use our existing resources more effectively…. It is time for all interested parties to look for new approaches within the limits of budgetary realities." That sentiment was past due, but did Wilson and Mulroney follow through?

In a word, NO. The question of how much money the federal government transfers to the provinces and under what conditions is integrally tied to two other questions: How should tax moneys be collected and shared in Canada? And who should be responsible for which social and educational programs? These questions were first asked systematically in the late 1930s by the Rowell-Sirois Commission on federal-provincial relations. Its recommendations at least identified the fundamental contradiction of the Canadian constitutional structure: the areas of taxation open to the provinces were (and are) much more limited than those open to Ottawa, but the provinces are responsible for the largest spending areas. Specifically, social and educational spending are under provincial jurisdiction. Rowell-Sirois could not come up with anything better than to recommend the transfer of jurisdiction over much social spending to Ottawa, a proposition that most of the provinces, and especially Ontario and Quebec, repeatedly rejected.

In place of the wholesale rejigging of the constitution's fiscal arrangements that Rowell-Sirois recommended, Ottawa and the provinces worked out a series of tax-rental agreements and agreements to share the costs of programs such as medicare. Most of those arrangements reflected the heady optimism of the times during which they were made. Now, however, Ottawa's huge debt burden forces it to look for ways to save money, and one obvious way to do that is to transfer more and more of the costs of the "shared-cost" programs on to the provinces. Ottawa's slice of medicare and higher education spending has been greatly reduced; the burden on the provinces has been greatly increased.

Canada badly needs a thorough overhaul of the system, and the Wilson position paper projected such an overhaul, but no overhaul was ever carried out. The Mulroney government did not initiate a serious and prolonged series of negotiations with the provinces with a view to reforming the tax structure, the social spending mechanism, and the means by which funds are transferred. No attempts were made to identify overlap and duplication, so no steps towards eliminating this obvious area of waste were seriously contemplated. The process would have required an effort at least as sustained, and possibly as painful, as that which Mulroney poured into constitutional reform. Indeed, it might have required its own set of constitutional amendments. But it might well have solved underlying and systemic problems that the entire country is now paying for. Instead, the government got mired in the Meech and Charlottetown fiascos.

This does not mean that the Mulroney government did nothing about federal-provincial transfers. Towards the end of its mandate, in 1990, the government unilaterally capped transfer payments to the provinces, a move it extended for a further two years in its 1991 budget. Given that virtually all provincial governments had also run up huge debts and depended more than ever on these payments, the net result was to download a significant portion of the burden for higher education, medicare, and other programs on the provincial taxpayer, who is, after all, the same man or woman who pays federal taxes. It also, naturally, exacerbated federal-provincial relations precisely because it was unilateral. One of the first things to emerge at the first First Ministers' meeting after the federal election of October 25, 1993, was a proposal that a thorough study of taxation and the federal-provincial fiscal relationship be carried out as soon as possible. Thus, it will fall to Jean Chrétien's Liberals to do the job. We'll see.

(7) *The deficit*: The Mulroney record on deficit reduction is decidedly mixed. Deficit reduction was going to be a major government priority, but it didn't turn out that way. The fact is, the Mulroney/Campbell Tories ran up the largest peacetime debt and deficit, by any measure, in Canadian history. In 1984–85 the deficit was $38.5 billion, nearly 5 per cent of the Gross Domestic Product (GDP); in 1993–94 the deficit reached well over $40 billion, though it had fallen to just over 4 per cent of GDP. The cumulative national debt stood at $206 billion in 1984–85, or 46 per cent of GDP, and was well over $450 billion, or 63 per cent of GDP, in 1991–92. In 1992–93 Ottawa had to set aside $43 billion just to pay interest on the national debt. If interest payments on the national debt are set aside, the federal government has actually run a surplus each year since the late 1980s; it is these debt charges that put Ottawa into the red each year.

There are at least three reasons why the deficit/debt picture is still bleak even after nine years of Tory efforts to get it down (and countless over-optimistic projections on the part of the Tory finance ministers as to when it would be under control). They are: political timidity; the Bank of Canada's high-interest-rate policies of the late 1980s and early 1990s; and the recession of 1990–93.

Whatever the ultimate validity of Keynesian economics, it has been embraced by virtually every Western government since World War Two. One of its cardinal principles is that budgets need to be balanced over a business cycle, and not annually. The Canadian government gave notice that it was going to run its financial affairs along Keynesian lines in its White Paper on Employment and Incomes in 1945. But in order to do that, governments have to be willing to run surpluses in boom times to pay for the deficits they accumulate during recessions. The theory is that the deficits contribute to job creation (either by government or in the private sector) as the economic cycle reaches bottom, but that the private sector takes up the job-creation slack as the economic cycle curves back up again.

The theory is simple: the practice much harder. To begin with, as was indicated in the first chapter, the "business cycle" is a somewhat illusive reality. It is much easier to detect after the fact than when one is in its midst. One simply cannot tell if a change is a blip or the start of a trend. But even if one had perfect twenty-twenty foresight and knew which phase of the cycle one was in at any particular moment, the necessary flexibility in designing theoretically appropriate economic policies is severely restricted when governments chisel spending programs into stone and cast compensation levels into concrete. For example, family allowances were automatically increased to keep pace with the inflation of the 1970s and 1980s, but if strict Keynesian philosophy had been followed, at the very least they would have been frozen and probably should have been reduced during periods of economic expansion.

The same ought to have applied to all other forms of federal government payouts to individuals, with the probable exception of means-related payments such as the Guaranteed Income Supplement paid to pensioners. That is simply what counter-cyclical economic policy means.

Of course, nothing remotely approaching that was undertaken. To have tried would have caused a major uproar for which the Tory government clearly had no stomach. It signalled its timidity early on when it backed down on the perfectly reasonable proposal to partially de-index the OAS in the spring of 1985. That proposal was timid enough; had the government announced a wholesale cutback in payouts to restore payments to levels comparable to those that existed in the pre-Diefenbaker period (adjusted for inflation), on the assumption that Canada was out of recession and headed into economic expansion, the uproar would have been unprecedented. At no time in the first four years of his mandate did Mulroney indicate his willingness to take such bold action, even though he had the biggest majority in Canadian history. Thus, the Mulroney government's political timidity must be blamed as one cause of his failure to deliver on serious deficit reduction.

The problem of political timidity was compounded by the Bank of Canada's high-interest-rate policy under Governor John Crow. Crow was appointed to a seven-year term in 1986. As governor, he had (as all governors have) considerable leeway to set Canada's monetary policy, which means, in effect, to control the money supply of the nation. Although the governor of the Bank reports to the minister of finance, Bank policy is supposed to be set at arm's length from the government to keep politics out of the decision-making process. It is nevertheless possible for the minister of finance to give informal guidance and advice to the governor of the Bank and, if the governor disagrees, to issue a formal directive that ought to bring the governor's resignation. At bottom it is the Government of Canada and not the governor of the Bank of Canada that is responsible for the nation's fiscal policy.

Crow was an inflation fighter. He was determined to "wrestle inflation to the ground" and cure this chronic disease that had been attacking the nation's economic stability since the late 1960s at least. His target was nothing less than zero inflation. To achieve it, he maintained a policy of high interest rates. The cost of a high-interest-rate policy is that people stop buying big-ticket items that they have to borrow to purchase. For example, consumers don't want to pay high interest rates on mortgages and car loans, so they put off house and car purchases. In addition, when interest rates go up on loans, they also raise the cost of government borrowing. That means that the government had to offer high interest rates on its debt instruments (Canada Savings Bonds, Government of Canada bonds, etc.), which meant its own cost of servicing its debt increased accordingly.

Crow's task was certainly complicated by the confused and confusing international monetary picture of the late 1980s and early 1990s. The U.S. Federal Reserve Board also kept its discount rate high to fight inflation, and the German bank rate was raised as one means of stabilizing the Deutschmark at a time when Germany was beginning to pour billions of Deutschmarks into the development of formerly Communist eastern Germany. A Bank of Canada governor would be irresponsible if he or she allowed Canadian interest rates to fall to the point where foreign and Canadian investors could get better rates of return from the purchase of, say, American debt instruments. Crow's room to manoeuvre was therefore constrained; nevertheless, he did have *some* room.

Crow succeeded in helping to wrestle inflation near to zero; he was aided in his crusade by high unemployment and a steep recession. If the government disagreed with a policy that was making its own deficit fighting so much more difficult, it did not say so. It certainly made no move to remove Crow. Our conclusion, therefore, is that the government agreed with his priorities and was prepared to see the deficit and the debt increase as part of the cost of fighting inflation, even when there were ample signs that inflation had been brought under control.

In late 1990, Canada joined most of the other Western industrialized countries in entering the second worst recession since the end of World War Two. Only a fool or an ignoramus would suggest that a country of just 27 million people, with a productive capacity so heavily dependent on the export trade, could avoid going into recession when the world's economic giants — the United States, Japan, Germany, the United Kingdom — were going into recession as well. There is some evidence that John Crow's tight money policy pushed Canada into recession earlier than might otherwise have happened, but the reality Canadians still have trouble facing is that even though the Canadian economy is much less heavily dependent on the extraction and export of natural products than it was, say, in the late 1950s, hewing wood and drawing water is still a significant part of what Canadians do. And whenever recessions happen, economies that are significantly resource-based enter them quicker, stay in them longer, and experience them more deeply than those that are industrially based. In any case, unemployment in Canada, which had finally drifted down into high single digits after the debacle of 1981–83, rose steeply once again. As a result, the federal tax take declined, welfare and UI payouts climbed, and the deficit ballooned once again.

The bottom line on the deficit is this: yes, the Mulroney deficit grew much more slowly than the Trudeau deficit had, and federal government spending over the nine Mulroney/Campbell years averaged less than the rate of inflation; but even the staunchest defender of the Tory regime would be hard-pressed to make the case either that the government did absolutely all it could to reduce program spending, or that it attempted to deal with the underlying structural problems such as a chronically high unemployment rate that have made deficit fighting so difficult in Canada.

Whatever its record of tackling the debt, unemployment, and other issues, the Mulroney Tories get good marks in three other areas that impact directly on economic growth and development — trade, foreign investment, and immigration. Although no fan of free trade at the start of his mandate, Mulroney was quickly convinced that changing global trade patterns made a free-trade agreement with the United States necessary. To his credit his government negotiated a treaty with the United States and defended it in a hard-fought election in 1988 that was dominated by both demagoguery and outright lies perpetrated by its opponents. Similarly, the self-inflicted damage first perpetrated by the Pearson Liberals in trying to throttle foreign investment was largely undone when the Foreign Investment Review Agency was dismantled and turned into Investment Canada. Finally, the government accepted arguments that Canada's population base was too narrow and greatly increased immigration quotas.

Even these moves in the right direction were not well executed, however. Free trade with the United States was and is vitally necessary. So, too, is Canada's participation in the North American Free Trade Agreement (NAFTA), another Mulroney initiative. But promises that were made to help people displaced as a direct result of the FTA were not kept. Even though FTA opponents had no need for facts or evidence in making their appeal, the absence of government action helped the opponents of free trade continue to spread the myth that the recession Canada went through after 1990 was largely generated by the FTA. And although immigration is also necessary for a country such as Canada, few efforts were made, other than media commercials extolling the virtues of tolerance and understanding, to prepare the Canadian people for the increase in visible minorities that has resulted. A thorough review of Canada's policy of promoting "multiculturalism" was also long overdue and was not carried out in the Mulroney years.

So the Mulroney economic record is mixed. Part of the blame must be placed directly at Mulroney's own door, especially since he was so closely involved with the making of finance policy in the first four years of his term in office. But part is also attributable to factors beyond his control, particularly the worldwide recession of 1990–93 and the changing nature of the global economy. No honest critic of the Tories can ignore the fact that the world is a vastly more difficult and complex place today than it was even in 1984 when the Tories came to power. High-speed data links, computers, and satellite communication now make it possible for manufacturers to separate out the unskilled parts of the productive process and spin them offshore to low-wage areas while maintaining the integrity of the rest of the process. That means that low-skilled jobs are flowing into low-wage areas around the globe and countries such as Canada are feeling the results. The trick is to ensure that the disappearance of low-skill, low-wage jobs is matched by increases in high-skill, high-wage jobs. It is simply too early to tell whether or not Tory trade and economic policies will lead to that result.

One thing is certain: as halting as their effort sometimes was, the Mulroney Tories at least made the effort. They succeeded in placing deficit and debt issues at the top of the nation's economic agenda. They reversed a long and perverse Canadian trend towards looking upon government ownership as a panacea for job salvation or a way of achieving pseudo-nationalistic goals. They opened Canada more fully to the global tides of trade and investment that flowed increasingly strongly in the 1980s and early 1990s, and they began the process of reform of the social spending system that the next government is certain to complete — certain because it has no choice. If the Tories never accomplished anything else, at least they pointed out that the old emperor had no clothes on. Had they stopped at that, they would have done the nation a real service. But they did not; Mulroney could not resist the temptation to return the nation to constitutional fiddling.

Whatever the Tory economic record, a great deal of the government's time and effort, not to mention its creative capacity, went not to ensure far-reaching reforms of the economic structure, but to renovate the constitution. At a time when Canadians should have been drawn together, and behind the Mulroney government (a government, after all, to which they had given a strong mandate) in a campaign to regain the prosperity, stability, and economic optimism that marked the first decade or so of the postwar era, they were being driven apart in a wrangle over the constitution. The Meech Lake and Charlottetown processes opened deep wounds among Canadians, or further widened existing gaps, when the real energy of the nation should have been focused on basic economic reform. If Brian Mulroney had taken a lesson from Canadian history, he might have realized at the very start of his mandate that Canada and Canadians have never taken kindly to political leaders who have tried to shape their souls and lead them down the paths of ideological, constitutional, or any other sort of public virtue. He might have discovered that building "Canadianism" was a no-win proposition. He ought to have known that it was not part of his mandate, that no one outside a handful of nationalists in Quebec really cared, and that it was the farthest thing from the minds of the vast majority of the Canadian people who voted for him on September 8, 1984.

Historians and political scientists will long argue over which factors produced the peculiar electoral results of October 25, 1993; every election is a complex event, in that voters are almost always moved to act as they do by a variety of issues, personalities, individual desires, and so on. But one thing seems clear: the Tory débâcle followed closely the pattern set by the defeat of the "Yes" campaign in the referendum on the Charlottetown Accord almost exactly one year earlier on October 26, 1992. In that referendum, both Quebec and the West strongly rejected the accord; in the election of 1993 both Quebec and the West strongly rejected the Tories. In effect, Kim Campbell fought a two-front war to hold on to the Quebec/western Canada power base that had provided Mulroney with his two majority governments. She had little real chance at success precisely because of the stance Mulroney had taken both on the need for a new constitutional *modus vivendi* and on the shape that the deal should take. Put simply, his efforts on behalf of Quebec had led Tory voters in the West to desert the party in favour of Reform, while his failure to deliver on promises he had made to Quebec nationalists such as Lucien Bouchard prompted many who had voted Tory in Quebec in 1984 and 1988 to vote for the Bloc.

In plunging into the dangerous game of constitutional politics, Brian Mulroney placed himself in a situation where he was certain to lose. The Meech Lake Accord of 1987 had, at one time or another, been accepted by all ten provincial governments and the federal government. And yet it is clear from public opinion polls, the popularity of Newfoundland premier Clyde Wells and Manitoba Cree leader Elijah Harper, that in English-speaking Canada Meech Lake was rejected by the people even though their leaders backed it. Though it was a fluke of politics that the Meech Lake Accord died, the lesson was clear: Brian Mulroney should have let the matter rest. He did not; perhaps he could not. Two years after the failure of Meech, Mulroney was back with a new and much broader set of proposals designed to meet the needs of just about every interest group in the nation. But this time criticism about the process was met head-on by the holding of a national referendum; unless the people in all ten provinces endorsed the Charlottetown Accord, it would fail. Mulroney was praised in some quarters for this, but in reality he had little choice, since Quebec, Alberta, and British Columbia were going to hold provincial referenda anyway. The democratization of the constitutional approval process made that process somewhat more palatable, but not the result — Charlottetown was defeated in six provinces out of ten and passed in Ontario by only 10,000 votes.

Thus, Mulroney committed two cardinal errors for which Kim Campbell paid dearly. First, he forgot that, when elected in 1984, he had not been given a mandate to continue with constitutional tinkering. He had, instead, been elected to put the Canadian economy back on track, clean up the sloppy and extravagant practices of the Liberals, and begin a thorough reform of the social welfare system and federal-provincial fiscal relations. Second, he had followed in the footsteps of Trudeau, Pearson, and Diefenbaker in trying to tell Canadians who and what they were and in trying to redefine their relationship to each other and to the Canadian national state. He tried, in other words, to maintain the national government's role as cheerleader and prime agent of the Canadian national identity. In so doing he destroyed his credibility as a man who might have led the nation into a new economic era.

Brian Mulroney had said little about the constitution in the 1984 election campaign. In a speech in Sept-Iles, Quebec, however, he pledged to get Quebec's signature on the Canadian constitution with "honour and enthusiasm." It was wholly appropriate that the speech that announced Mulroney was taking Canada down the wrong road was written by his good friend Lucien Bouchard, soon to become his bitter enemy as leader of the Bloc. Indeed, the relationship between Mulroney and Bouchard is a small and dramatic tableau that illustrates the larger folly of attempting to tell Canadians who they are instead of simply minding the store.

Quebec's signature was missing from the constitution because at the time the agreement regarding patriation and the Charter was hammered out between Ottawa and the provinces in 1981, Quebec's separatist leader, René Lévesque, refused to sign it. From that refusal a myth was created by, among others, Quebec's nationalist media (and most Quebec journalists evidently hew closely to the nationalist line), that Lévesque and Quebec had been stabbed in the back, or worse, by Trudeau and the leaders of the Anglophone provinces. Thus it would fall to Mulroney to right the wrong that was falsely claimed to have been done, and to secure the Quebec government's signature on a new constitutional accord. That the Quebec nationalists' version of Canadian history was based on a fairy tale seemed not to matter to Mulroney. Canadians, however, including Quebeckers who no longer need fairy tales, need only ask themselves the following question: If Lévesque was truly a separatist, would he ever have agreed to a constitution that would have strengthened Quebec's position *within* Canada and Quebec's ties *to* Canada? If Lévesque were truly a separatist, his presence at the negotiating table was itself evidence of *mauvaise foi*. But we have already seen that he only looked like a separatist and talked like a separatist. Really, he was just a sovereignty-associationist. But then, in the mythic world of Quebec fairy tales, if he was not deep down a separatist of some sort, why had he devoted his life since 1968 to the separatist cause and why is he so revered by separatists today as a nationalist hero? The Quebec media simply cannot have it both ways, at least not in real life.

The fact that Quebec separatists were caught in mortal coils of their own making did not oblige the Prime Minister of Canada to enter the turmoil. So why did Mulroney do it? One answer that a senior minister would give long after was that "events took over." That is an excuse, not a reason. Although some Quebeckers clearly felt aggrieved about the events of 1981–82 (some, of course, did not), they were not exactly demonstrating in the streets. If anything, they, like other Canadians, were working, saving, spending, and investing their way out of the recession. There was no sign that constitution fixing was the first thing they thought about when they opened their eyes each morning.

Nevertheless, having helped to create and enthusiastically, if not honourably, embraced it, Mulroney had to put it to rest. He had too much riding on it not to. He had, in essence, built a power base in Quebec on the backs of separatists with the promise that Quebec's aspirations could and would be fulfilled under a Tory government. He either did not believe Trudeau, who had declared that no government of Canada could treat with such people, or he did not care. But there was a major obstacle he had to overcome; Quebec's demands were simply not acceptable to the rest of Canada.

In the years following the patriation of the constitution the Parti Québécois government in Quebec City was replaced by a Liberal government under Robert Bourassa. The Liberals had declared a number of irreducible conditions for acquiescing in that patriation. Among those was a clause in the constitution directing that Quebec be recognized as a "distinct society" and that the Quebec government be recognized as possessing a constitutional responsibility for keeping it that way. That appeared to many Canadians as a *carte blanche* to pass whatever legislation the government of Quebec might declare to be necessary to preserve the French nature of the province, no matter whose rights were violated in the process. In the fall of 1988, about a year after the conclusion of the Meech Lake Accord and before it was fully ratified, Bourassa gave a dramatic demonstration of what that could mean when his government introduced Bill 178 into the Quebec National Assembly. It used the "notwithstanding" clause provided for by the constitution to set aside the Charter's provisions regarding free speech so that Quebec could override a Supreme Court of Canada decision that Quebec legislation banning the use of English on outdoor commercial signs was illegal. Many English-speaking Canadians asked themselves how much more of such outrageous behaviour they could expect to see if Meech Lake was adopted. Manitoba premier Gary Filmon decided not to put the Meech Lake Accord to the vote in his legislature in the certain knowledge that Bill 178 would cause the defeat of Meech in Manitoba and thus its death.

With the Meech Lake proposals, the Prime Minister of Canada had said to Quebec: "What price do the federal government and the other nine provinces have to pay to secure Quebec's assent to the patriation of the constitution?" — its assent, in short, to an event that had already happened. The manner of the request conveyed the impression that Brian Mulroney and the premiers were admitting culpability in an unspeakable act and asking for Quebec's forgiveness. Thus the entire Meech Lake charade was presented to the Canadian people as a morality play in which the federal government was riding to save the virtue of the people of Canada and to rescue Quebec, the quintessential victim of Confederation, from the dungeon into which it had been cast.

The simple fact is that meeting Bourassa's demands would have destroyed Canada as it has existed since 1867. Bourassa has been hailed in many quarters as a great federalist, but his record shows that since the late 1960s he has regularly flirted with separatism, that he has *never* stood up to the nationalists (possibly because he agreed with much of what they said), and that his so-called faith in federalism was based on the extent to which federalism was "profitable" to Quebec. The irreducible demands that Bourassa listed as the price for Quebec's support of constitutional patriation were little different in form or substance from the positions that prominent separatists such as Claude Morin (a real-life separatist when he was not also acting as an RCMP informer) had been putting forward for years. In fact, they were little different from those that Lévesque himself had advanced at the time the constitutional discussions were taking place in 1981. By that point, after all, Lévesque had had his referendum (held in the spring of 1980) and had been defeated; all he had left to advance the cause of separation, a cause he may well have deeply believed in, was "*étapisme*," originally Morin's brain-child. *Étapisme* was to be secession not in one bold stroke, but slowly, in step-by-step fashion, and in such a manner that Quebec would incrementally withdraw from the rest of Canada, which would awake some day to find Quebec effectively gone. *Étapisme* held no terrors for Brian Mulroney. Mulroney was a deal-maker and an oft-proclaimed master of bringing parties together who might otherwise be at each other's throats. Bourassa could surely be accommodated, and Mulroney's place in Canadian history — and the Tories' hold on Quebec — would be assured.

The problem was, Quebec's demands have been escalating since the onset of the Quiet Revolution in the 1960s. There has never been room for any compromise that did not increase Quebec's power or its revenues. The Quebec game was to demand everything under the sun, justified or not, in the name of *la survivance*, and see what happened. Time after time Quebec placed demands for new powers or new revenues on the table, justifying those demands solely on the grounds that it was the "homeland" of Canadian Francophones. Homeland it most assuredly was and is, but in itself that justifies nothing. And when those demands were not met, as they could not be without changing the basic shape of the entire federation, then Quebec invariably scuttled the process. It did so with the Fulton proposals of 1961. It did so with the Fulton-Favreau arrangement of 1964. It did so with the proposed Victoria Charter of 1971. And why? Because Quebec's chattering classes, separatist through and through, supported by its equally nationalist media, refused to make any lasting, long-term commitment to Canada that might be construed as even semi-permanent. And to have accepted any one of these formulae would have entailed such a commitment. More important, it would have written *finis* to the process of *étapisme*. That, they could not accept at all.

As in any modern Western society, there is a great gulf in Quebec between the daily needs and aspirations of the people and the desires of the intellectuals, the academics, and the media élites. What Quebeckers want, at heart, is what virtually all North Americans want — financial security and the possibility of a better economic future. Macdonald and Cartier knew that, as did Laurier and King. But if challenged to express their understandable allegiance to their culture and language in absolute terms (i.e., do you, or do you not, want to remain French?), pretty well all Francophone Quebeckers will of course, proclaim that allegiance in terms that are unmistakable and that can only be defined within particular political structures. When they do that, it makes compromise of the type that Mulroney specialized in much more difficult. In essence, then, the very act of entering into the process made it all but impossible for the process to succeed.

When a group of people who perceive themselves to be a threatened, or oppressed, or deprived minority are asked by the majority what they desire, they will almost always lay their demands on the table in terms that are absolute, uncompromising, and extreme. They will ask for the maximum in the hopes of getting anything at all ("Since you ask, let me tell you *everything* I need") because they see their survival in absolute terms and demand absolute guarantees of cultural (or linguistic, or religious) security. The Quebec government did this in the months leading up to the Meech Lake Accord. Later the Quebec government was joined by a plethora of minority and special-interest groups to repeat the process in the months leading up to the Charlottetown Accord. That, too, practically guaranteed failure. This was particularly apparent in a document entitled *A Quebec Free to Choose* issued by the Quebec Liberal party's Allaire Committee (headed by Jean Allaire) in March 1991 and later endorsed by that party. The report called for a total restructuring of Canada, stripping Ottawa of virtually all its power and giving Quebec total authority over a wide range of legislative areas from the environment to communications. If Quebeckers ever believed that the Allaire Report could form the basis for a serious discussion with either Ottawa or the other provinces over constitutional change, they were dreaming in technicolour. The demands made by the Allaire Report were as arrogant as they were silly and not worth five minutes of anyone's time. They would have formed the basis not for any discussion over the future shape of Canada but for the dismemberment of a nation: *étapisme* with a federalist face. Had Ottawa ever taken them seriously and sat down with Quebec to discuss them, there would probably have been an armed revolt in English-speaking Canada. And yet, there they were: adopted by the governing Quebec Liberals as the roadmap to guide the Quebec government in any discussions it might have with the rest of the country. As an example of demanding the sun and the moon for openers, the report will long remain a classic, especially since the Charlottetown Accord fell so far short of the demands of the Allaire Report. Had the Allaire Report been slightly less ridiculous (and, therefore, something that Ottawa might have taken more seriously) it would have provided a prime example of constitutional brinksmanship.

There is a way to avoid such problems, of course — don't ask people to frame their demands. Leave fundamental questions about language, culture, religion, and so on, alone. Recognize and accept that there is not now (and never has been) a Canadian consensus on non-economic matters. This is partly because of the diversity of the Canadian people but mostly because there has never been a process in which Canadians have come together in agreement on a given set of constitutional principles. That latter course was not even thought of when Confederation was forged. Canada was to be a constitutional monarchy governed by a national (Dominion) government in the British tradition of social harmony, order, and a structured society. Nothing else was needed.

But after the defeat of the Meech Lake Accord, Brian Mulroney forged ahead once again. Having raised the constitutional cadaver once, he had to attempt a second time to breathe life into it, despite the fact that the Meech process had uncovered two major fault lines. First, it soon became painfully obvious that most ordinary people in English-speaking Canada had not agreed with their leaders about Meech Lake. At one time all ten provincial governments, the federal government, and the national opposition parties represented in the House of Commons — the Liberals and the NDP — had all endorsed the accord. Surely the nation was united as never before on a set of constitutional principles. But it was not. In time-honoured fashion the constitutional deal had been forged in secret and would be put before Parliament and the legislatures without elections or a referendum. There was nothing in this that deviated from past practice, but 1987 was not 1867. Many people in English-speaking Canada had begun to take democracy seriously and would no longer countenance constitutional change by means of the old methods of élite accommodation. They disagreed both with the substance of the accord and with the means that were being used to foist it on the nation.

The second major fault line was between Quebec's demand for special status and the belief of most English-speaking Canadians that no province should have powers greater than any other and that all Canadians must share equally in the protections of the Charter. Ordinarily, who would care about such arcane matters? Would the prevalence of one view over the other place any more food on the tables of Canadians, or provide a single new job? But once the process had been initiated and these matters of principle had been brought to the centre of the national arena, they became more than arcane positions; they became fundamental values, fixed in concrete and believed to set English-speaking Canadians off against Quebeckers for all time and in all important matters. Nonsense it was and is, but it was and is powerful nonsense.

And so Brian Mulroney charged his chief political rival, Joe Clark, with the task of binding up the nation's wounds. Only this time, it was proclaimed, the process would be more democratic, more inclusive; and it would address just about every grievance that every definable group of Canadians could bring forward. The "Charlottetown Accord process" degenerated into a national orgy of self-indulgence that eventually grafted the essence of the Meech Lake Accord on to a shopping list of demands from the West, from Aboriginals, from the political left, from the official multicultural community, from women, from the other provinces and territories, and from the business community (we hope we haven't left anyone off the list).

No wonder the Accord itself turned out to be little more than a smorgasbord of special political demands from a plethora of special-interest groups. There was not a genuine constitutional principle within miles. In trying to please everyone, the framers of Charlottetown had pleased almost no one and had violated the cardinal rule of Canadian accommodation — they had tried to impose from above their own definition of Canadianism on Canadians. The political leaders, the bureaucrats, and the expensive academic advisers who had helped them had tried to redesign the nation to fit their own definitions of what Canada ought to be. They had gathered virtually every myth that has ever been pronounced about Canada as a bilingual, binational, multicultural, kind, gentle, socially conscious, politically correct, moderate, accommodative, compromising, tolerant society and used those myths as the template for a new constitution. They wanted their Canada to be a society of all-embracing public virtue, watched over by a benevolent national government shorn of a portion of the vital economic powers that a national government must have to protect and advance the economic interests of its citizens.

In no way was that more obvious than in the writing of the so-called Canada Clause of the Charlottetown Accord. Designed to "guide the courts in their future interpretation of the entire Constitution, including the Canadian Charter of Rights and Freedoms" the clause sought to tell Canadians what sort of country Canada is. It declared that Canada is a democracy; that the governments of Aboriginal Canadians were "one of three orders of government in Canada"; that Quebec constituted "within Canada a distinct society"; that Canadians were committed to bilingualism, ethnic diversity, both individual and "collective human rights" (a neat trick!), and the equality of men and women. It also proclaimed that Canadians believed provinces to be equal while at the same time recognizing "their diverse characteristics." The Canada Clause was so full of contradictions, saw-offs, compromises of the uncompromisable, and squared circles that it confused far more than it clarified. Macdonald, Laurier, King, and St. Laurent would have been appalled by it. It was a mess and it deserved the drubbing that Canadian people gave it on October 26, 1992. Their "No" was a "Yes" to what Canada really was. Only the politicians and their servants failed to notice.

Canadians rightly blamed Mulroney. It was indeed his fault, for messing with the constitution in the first place. But it was not his fault that his ministers and the premiers could not forge a constitutional consensus. No one can "forge" a constitutional consensus if the people themselves have not reached such a consensus. In Canada, the people have never done so because to do so would be publicly to disavow cherished principles that do not matter one iota in daily life, but that are dusted off and bowed down to every now and then — and worshipped when the occasion seems to warrant it.

In the meantime, five years had been wasted. Had the governing Tories put the time and money devoted to Meech and Charlottetown into improving Canada's economic structure, or rejigging its federal-provincial fiscal relations, or reforming its social welfare system, or anything useful, much positive change might have emerged. The nation might have come together on the means of achieving greater economic growth even though Canadians proba- bly can never come together to agree on a set of constitutional principles. But opportunities were missed, and the Tories left Canada more disunited and in more trouble than when they start- ed. True, Mulroney had only inherited a process initiated by Diefenbaker, an attempt to place the search for public virtue at the top of the federal government's national agenda. But he alone was responsible for taking that process much farther than his predeces- sors did. Thus his deplorable record on the constitution more than offset his genuine but modest achievement on the economy. The chickens came home to roost, as they always do, and the result was the virtual annihilation of his party under the leadership of his successor.

6
Fixing It

A spate of books has flooded the bad-news market lately. Any number of journalists, academics, politicians, and just plain folks have seen that our economic and political affairs have gone sour. That is the easy part. It is more difficult to say, as we have tried to do in this book, *why* things have gone wrong. It is even more difficult to figure out what might be done to ameliorate our present discontents — if anything. Before even attempting to outline, in broad terms, what setting a new course for the ship of state entails, it is necessary to have a clear understanding of the course that has brought us, decks awash, so near to foundering.

Several times we have said that the quest for public virtue — for an uplifting definition of true Canadianism, for a clear and explicit national identity — was a foolish enterprise. Our thinking has been chiefly historical: Canada was not established for patriotic purposes, but for other reasons. And when politicians have tried to graft new branches on an old stem, the results have sapped our energies and brought forth bitter fruit. There is a reason why the quest for national unity, unhyphenated Canadianism, and all the other "isms" that seduce the unwary into the dreamlands of collectivist fantasy have failed. Our first task, in this chapter, then, is to provide, if not a causal explanation of what went wrong, then a critical interpretation.

Northrop Frye was one of the great interpreters of our cultural landscape as well as a scholar of ecumenical fame and importance. In the preface to *The Bush Garden*, a collection of some of his writings on Canadian culture, he established a distinction that is of some significance to our interpretation of Canada's political woes. There he drew a sharp division between identity and unity. The question of identity, which we have expanded to include other matters grouped under the collectivist category of public virtue, is, according to Frye, "primarily a cultural and imaginative question, and there is always something vegetable about the imagination, something sharply limited in range." Identity *cannot* be a national issue because it is by nature a local one, where the locale can be as small as an individual soul or as wide as a region of the mind. "What can there be in common," Frye asked, "between an imagination nurtured on the prairies, where it is a center of consciousness diffusing itself over a vast flat expanse stretching to the remote horizon, and one nurtured in British Columbia, where it is in the midst of gigantic trees and mountains leaping into the sky all around it, and obliterating the horizon everywhere?" The answer is: very little.

One finds identities expressed most clearly in works of art, in literature, and in the stories told by historians. The contrasts can be seen clearly by juxtaposing the art of Emily Carr with that of

William Kurelek, or of both with the work of Cornelius Krieghoff or Tom Thomson. Compare the opening words of W.O. Mitchell's *Who Has Seen the Wind* and Margaret Atwood's *The Edible Woman*, and the contrast appears in yet another form. Or compare the subtle evocations of place by two of Canada's most celebrated historians as found in the opening words of their most famous books. First, Donald Creighton:

> When, in the course of a September day in 1759, the British made themselves the real masters of the rock of Quebec, an event of apparently unique importance occurred in the history of Canada. There followed rapidly the collapse of French power in North America and the transference of the sovereignty of Canada to Great Britain; and these acts in the history of the northern half of the continent may well appear decisive and definitive above all others.

So begins *The Empire of the St. Lawrence*. W.L. Morton evokes another image entirely in *Manitoba: A History*:

> In mid-August, 1612, the western shores of Hudson Bay lay as they had lain for unnumbered years, level and low, unmarked by headland and unrelieved by rearward hills. The rocky beaches from their ragged crests shelved slowly out beneath the shoal waters, running in their brief season's sunlight or surging sullenly beneath the quick fogs of summer. No high land was to be seen, and no deep water found. Save for the cry of gulls along the breakers' wash or dash of caribou across the landward plains, the shores were still with the stillness of the sub-Arctic, and silent as their prehistory is silent.

Frye's point is illustrated by these two passages and may be reiterated in the statement that Canadian identities are nourished by a sense of locality. And everyone lives someplace.

This does not mean that there are no imaginative forms common to the whole country, but that whenever they have been found, they turn out to be common to other cultures as well. And being common to Canadians and to non-Canadians, these forms can hardly constitute any particular cultural identity. At best they serve as archetypes for the human soul, but that is not our concern here.

From all the evidence, then, Canadians have various identities — as many as there are locales to sustain them. Let us consider what this means, in simplified form, by confining the discussion to English-speaking Canadians. The popular sense of locale is nourished by common stories, and stories belong to the inwardness of human life: they convey meanings. In western Canada, for example, what began as a political complaint over land policy or an economic objection to discriminatory freight rates can become the constituent element of a story that reveals a meaning. This transformation of fact or narrative into a typical example distinguishes history from myth. The two forms overlap to some degree: myths often contain a great deal of history, and historiography is often structured to conform with mythic conventions. Even so, history generally aims at telling what happened, whereas, as Frye once said, myth aims at telling what happens all the time. In discussing the National Energy Program, for instance, we said that for many Albertans it was part of a pattern; for some it was of a piece with the disallowance of Social Credit legislation fifty years earlier. There was, of course, no historical link between the two acts; the link was mythic and the reality it expressed was one of regional identity. This being so, it makes no sense to point out the lack of evidence of historical connection. The same kind of disjunction between myth and historical fact is even more apparent in Quebec. The difference with Quebec, of course, is that for other reasons these stories have a political impact on the rest of us and so must be taken seriously, not as history but as a source of political disorder.

It is true enough that no work of imaginative literature in Canada belongs among the great classics of Western civilization. But that simply means that we are aware of the social and historical setting of our literary artifacts. Canadian literature records what the Canadian imagination has experienced as meaningful, and it tells readers about those meanings in a way that nothing else can do. Whether or not Canadian imaginative writing is good literature is a question that can be answered by reference to formal canons of what literature is, but that question does not concern us. Like the clown's Audrey in *As You Like It*, it may be an ill-favoured thing, but it is our own. And being our own, even if graceless, it gives an undistorted voice to our imaginative experience. Chief among the questions literature answers is, as Frye remarked, "Where is here?" To which may be added a derivative one, "Who are we?" The short answer is: We are those who know where here is; they don't know because they are not from here but from there. The "knowledge" of we and they, of here and there, and of all the subsidiary things that are implied by this strange knowing is not an awareness of facts but an imaginative and participatory knowledge.

To put the point in more ordinary language, when someone says, "I am a Newfoundlander," or "I am a Westerner," or "*Je suis Québécoise,*" he or she means *something*. Specifically, each is making an imaginative or metaphorical identification of place and meaning. Each is answering the question: "Where is (my) here?" The answer is an expression of identity.

Unity, as distinct from identity, Frye said, "is national in refer-

ence, international in perspective, and rooted in a political feeling." This distinction is useful, though Frye himself was not always
careful about its use. Later in the book from which we have been
quoting, for instance, Frye summarized his impressions of the
Canadian imagination as being characterized by "what we may
provisionally call a garrison mentality." There is a contradiction
here, insofar as a Canadian imagination made articulate a national
identity. As Dennis Duffy pointed out in *Gardens, Covenants, Exiles*,
his study of the literature of Upper Canada and Ontario, "Canada"
as a symbol of identity was centred in the Loyalist heartland, the
wedge of land south of the Shield between the valley of the
Ottawa River and Lake Huron. Imaginatively, it was indeed filled
with garrisons concerned with survival and hanging on. In that
locale, Duffy showed, the myth of exile (from the American
colonies), covenant (loyalty to the Crown), and return to a garden
(the transformed wilderness) fully expressed the regional identity
of "Canada."

Duffy's analysis clarified a crucial but unanalysed assumption of
Frye. Canada, the imaginative reality, belonged to the experience
of the Loyalist heartland. Like all such experiences, it was local.
Canada, the political reality, what Duffy called the "noblest product Ontario had to offer to the rest of Canada," was "sectionalized,
misappropriated, its rhetoric employed to justify the smashing of
the alternative Canada that had sprung from the Métis experience." Duffy did not enlarge on what the Métis-inspired alternative might have been. He did, however, identify it with the West,
which suggested that an ampler Canada that did not betray itself
was somehow linked to the export of the noblest product of
Ontario. He did not dwell on what made that "vision of nationhood" noble, nor did he say what he meant by vision. We can,
however, make the following tentative conclusion: Canada, the

imaginative reality centred in the Loyalist heartland, became Canada the political reality. In the process, it betrayed its own regional identity and destroyed the possibility of an alternative political reality that Duffy identified in an unclear way with the Métis experience and that in any event was located in the West.

Clearly, there is an ambiguity in the meaning of "Canada." Those who drew their sense of place from the imaginative Canada, the Loyalist heartland, as Frye did, implicitly identified that place with the political unit stretching from sea to sea, and from the river — the St. Lawrence River — to the ends of the earth (cf. Psalm 72:8), which meant not a vague emptiness off towards the North Pole, but the great lone land lying in a northwesterly direction beyond the river and Hudson Bay. To the imaginative Canadians, the ones of the garrison mentality, the ones who drew up the national motto, the West was the end of the earth, a "there" not a "here." Without even considering British Columbia or Quebec or the pluralities of Atlantic Canada, we see once again that Canada the political unit enjoys many identities.

At the same time, the insights of Duffy and Frye tell us a great deal about the meaning of those two great symbols of Loyalist regional identity, "Canadian nationalism" and "national unity." Both terms exemplify what Duffy called the use of rhetoric and what might be more accurately called propaganda or straightforward lying. That is, national unity and Canadian nationalism are symbols that express the regional identity of imaginative "Canada," the Loyalist heartland. This is why, for example, such "nationalist" policies as the National Energy Program and the "regulation" of foreign investment or imports of well-made foreign automobiles or combines look to many like attempts by the garrison to protect its own interests inside the central-Canadian industrial fort. Naturally enough, if you dwell within the fort, if you are an imaginative Canadian as well as a Canadian citizen, you will see things quite differently. The reality of such differences simply reinforces the importance we should accord to conflicting interests, ambitions, and opinions. We must, therefore, maintain Frye's distinction even against him: imaginative regional Canada, which is roughly southern Ontario, ought not be confused with federal, political Canada.

Our argument is the more compelling for being drawn from the work of a literary theorist who has almost nothing in common with us. The most obvious conclusion to be drawn from it is that any political activities designed to secure a Canadian national identity are doomed before they begin. Unity, to repeat, is political; identity is cultural — and it is plural in this country. Any attempt to use political means to forge a national identity is therefore akin to trying to carry water in a sieve. The most that can be achieved in politics in Canada is to try to provide conditions that may contribute to a sense of political unity. And chief among those conditions is prosperity.

Earlier in this book we spoke of economic fundamentalism. We do not use the term in a quasi-religious sense to express the belief that economic affairs are the most significant aspect of human life. We simply mean that the economy is the foundation of Canadian politics. Economic prosperity is fundamental, as nothing else is, to ensuring that Canadians have a sense of unity. This was the great insight of Macdonald and Cartier, of Laurier, King, and St. Laurent. On the basis of that understanding they were able to forge stable coalitions and bring a reasonable degree of harmony, or accord, to the country.

We have seen, however, that their insight was lost in what Edmund Burke would have called the "settled mismanagement" of Diefenbaker and Pearson and was utterly repudiated by Trudeau.

Even Mulroney, who had at least a vague appreciation of economic affairs, embarked on a fruitless attempt to bring Quebec into "the constitution." As if Quebec or any other province, region, or locale could ever be anywhere else! On the basis of Frye's distinction, it is clear that for a generation Canadians have been making what philosophers call a category mistake. We have been using politics to promote what it can never accomplish, a sense of who we are, of our identity.

What is perhaps even worse, we have been using the political instrument least likely to result in the generation of significant experiences and meaningful stories around which a larger identity might grow. No one beyond a few so-called constitutional experts can possibly have found the "constitutional odyssey," as Peter Russell called it, an edifying experience. The story of treachery, deception, manipulation, and appeals to fear is not the sort of tale one wishes to hand down from generation to generation. Even Russell's imagery is slightly misleading, for Odysseus actually made it home to Ithaka, and did so in only ten years, a much shorter time than Canadians have been at sea. At the same time as this futile generation-long quest for a national identity has failed, it has brought to light, in a way that Canadians have never had occasion to notice before, the essential nature and purpose of a constitution.

We saw that Brian Mulroney was more aware of the importance of prosperity to Canada than were any of his immediate predecessors. But his attitude was wrong. He thought the high calling of constitution writing was an up-market version of "Let's make a deal." That is why Andrew Cohen's account of the Meech Lake business was aptly titled *A Deal Undone*. But constitution making and deal making are different arts. Let us see why.

Any liberal democracy must assign great importance to freedom. But freedom looks different when it is considered from the point of view of economics than when it is looked at politically. In the economic view, freedom is simply a matter of interest; in the political view it is a matter of pride. And as we saw in connection with Trudeau, and with other fighting intellectuals on the left, pride and interest may conflict. But even if it does not lead to the perversities of a Trudeau, a matter of pride is, initially, a consideration that is not in one's interest. The short reason why Mulroney failed in his constitutional efforts, then, is that he addressed only the *interests* of Canadians and not their pride. This approach, as we saw, reached grotesque proportions in the so-called Canada Clause in the Charlottetown Accord, where virtually every interest under the sun was listed and, as if words alone could do the trick, was solemnly given constitutional significance.

The difficulty with pride and interest, as Harvey Mansfield has shown, lies in combining them. The difference between the two is clear enough: from the point of view of interest one must be frugal; but politics is the realm of pride, where individuals contend for prizes, honours, and recognition of their superiority. That is, politics seeks relief from the need to care for one's interests. Politics looks glamorous. In contrast, when politics is limited to the effort to satisfy various interests, it turns into the expanded collectivist housekeeping of the welfare state, which is the very definition of dependency. Why? Because it can easily appear to be, and in the short term may actually be, better to have one's interests catered to than to exercise freedom, which may be risky, costly, irksome, or dangerous. Why take a risk in the market when you can collect UI? Why bother to look for a job in Ontario or Alberta when the pain of saying "farewell to Nova Scotia, the sea-bound coast" is clearly so great and equalization payments to support fraudulent retraining schemes make it unnecessary anyhow?

There is an answer and it is one that redeems Canadians, as it does other people, from the necessity of remaining whiners. Before an individual can have an interest to promote or defend, he or she must have the pride — or the self-respect, which is the same thing — to *be* an individual. Freedom is necessary to one's interest because the very act of having an interest presupposes freedom. But if that is so, then when freedom must be defended it is in one's true interest to rise above one's immediate interest — in short, to sacrifice. Interest and pride can be allied when pride makes room for the pride of others, which is to say, their freedom. The overriding purpose of a constitution is to ensure that citizens can take pride in seeing that they have an interest in freedom — including the freedom of others to be stupid and prejudiced and in error.

Not all people have the political maturity to live under a constitution. Not everyone can accept limited government. Peter Russell, among others, has grave doubts about whether Canadians can constitute themselves as a sovereign people. In Cartier's notion of a political nation, or in Brown's New Nationality, something like the self-constitution of Canada was implied. Once upon a time, it seems, Canadians had what it took to accept a constitution. Moreover, they took pride in their achievement. That is why Duffy spoke of the *noblest* product Ontario had to offer the country. It was right and just for Canadians to take pride in that nobility. And nowadays, to the extent that Canadians are ashamed of their inability to constitute themselves as a sovereign people, they have offended their own pride. In that sense of shame resides hope. Let it not be said that the authors of this book are pessimists.

The lesson to be learned from our recent constitutional failures, we said, was that our politicians — Mulroney, Clark, Bourassa, and the rest — appealed to our interests and ignored our pride.

Constitutions, however, must take account of pride. In Canada, pride chiefly appears in the form of our various identities. There is no doubt we take pride in our identities more than we take pride in our political unity. This is not a flaw or a defect in the Canadian character. Rather it is a fact that is explained by the observation that identity need not deal with interests; identity, so to speak, is aristocratic. It sets "us" apart from "them" and demands, not requests, recognition. Unity, as a political and ultimately constitutional reality, concerns both pride and interest, and is, as we shall see, a more subtle concept than identity. The connection between pride and unity must be made through the constitution. We have seen time and again that no formulation of a national identity, no public proclamation of our collective virtue or of Canadianism, is possible. Such a "statement" can be made only through the constitution. But, as Mansfield pointed out, constitutions *can* do this because they are formal and formalities require sacrifices and sacrifices mean we have put aside our interests in order to satisfy our pride. Formalities in dress, for example, require a sacrifice of comfort: black-tie dinners are often less relaxed than burgers at McDonald's; "rangeland formal" is clearly a compromise. Likewise, formalities in politics require a sacrifice of leisure and often a sacrifice of income and so of interests.

The formal principle of Canadian political life, as of other liberal democratic regimes, is equality. No one can argue in such a regime in favour of two or several classes of citizens. Canadians will not listen to such arguments. That is why one speaks of equality of *rights*, for rights are formal and legal; the content, as distinct from the form, of rights will, of course, vary in terms of the choices, talents, and abilities of the holder. In no sense are rights merely wants. If they were, the strong — fighting intellectuals, for instance — could exercise them on behalf of the weak. And that would mean that rights flowed from weakness, not strength.

A second, and to a certain degree secondary, principle of Canadian political life is the principle of federalism or equality of the provinces. Neither principle has been highlighted in the constitutional rhetoric of the past few years. Instead, much talk has been devoted to "special status" and "collective rights." But these are matters that appeal solely to interests, not pride. Is it any wonder that Canadian citizens rejected them, either by speaking up against them or, when they had a chance, by voting them down? And they did so as a matter of pride. Bravo!

On the basis of the foregoing remarks, the conclusion to be drawn with respect to the two most important constitutional questions, namely the place of French Quebec and of the Aboriginal population, are clear enough. First of all, it seems clear that both the Quebec question and the Aboriginal question will return for our consideration. The Province of Quebec must hold an election shortly; the Bloc Québécois shows no signs of going away; the Royal Commission on Aboriginal Affairs will soon produce a report. Both these questions involve the formal conflict between universal rights and particular rights, the former being rights held by all individual citizens *qua* citizens, the latter being rights held by persons *qua* members of several collectives. In Europe, as we saw in chapter 1, the conflict took the form of a struggle between the state that extended equal protection to all and the nation that enjoyed its own particular virtue, purpose, myth, identity, and meaning.

If ever there was a conflict between pride and interest these two examples illustrate it in spades. For example, the position of French Quebec artists, each more nationalist than the next, paints the dilemma in day-glo colours: 40 per cent of Canada's "cultural" expenditures are disbursed in Quebec. Have they no shame? Have they no pride? Has Bourassa's *fédéralisme rentable* done its work that thoroughly? In *Deconfederation*, we proposed a solution that would address the pride, the *fierté*, of French Quebec as well as the interests of Canada. But French Quebec has not yet chosen independence, and it is highly unlikely that we can persuade it of the rightness of our solution now. We have a second-best solution, or at least a *modus vivendi*, to offer: just shut up about the constitution, eh?

One wonders, however, whether it is realistic to expect this. The leader of the Parti Québécois, Jacques Parizeau, has said: "If you ask me what will happen if we fail [in a referendum on independence] again, I will tell you: we will try again." For Mr. Parizeau, No does not mean No. But if that is the way he wants it, then surely, as an insightful editorial writer for the *Globe and Mail* observed, Yes cannot possibly mean Yes, either — at least not to the federalists. So it seems that the grave threat of a referendum to destroy the country is as toothless as the referendum on the Charlottetown Accord. The rest of us, outside the borders of the province, will be right in paying as much or as little attention to the results of a referendum as we do to the outcome of a provincial election.

In other words, while we can expect a lot of hot air from the mouths of Quebec politicians on either side of the independence question, we need pay absolutely no attention to it. Or if we do, it should be with the detachment of Brutus observing the choleric Cassius:

> Must I observe you? Must I stand and crouch
> Under your testy humour? By the gods,
> You shall digest the venom of your spleen,
> Though it do split you; for, from this day forth,
> I'll use you for my mirth, yea, for my laughter,
> When you are waspish.

The parallel between the Quebec and the Aboriginal questions is clear in the squabbles over the James Bay hydroelectric developments. The chief difference between the two is that Aboriginal "spirituality" is substituted for Quebec "nationalism." Of course, Aboriginal collectivities call themselves nations nowadays, but this is simply strategic rhetoric. As Tom Flanagan once observed, if the current terminology were accepted at face value, Canada would contain more "nations" than the rest of the world together. The average population of each would be less than 800.

The matter of Aboriginal "spirituality" can be put into context in a story recounted in Tocqueville's *Democracy in America*. In the concluding chapter to volume 1 of his classic study, Tocqueville reflected on the probable fate of the Aboriginals and their misfortune at coming into contact "with the most civilized nation in the world, and also, I would add, the greediest, at a time when they are themselves half barbarians, and to find masters in their instructors, having enlightenment and oppression brought to them together." Tocqueville was frank in his discussion of civilized and barbarian nations and of the brutality of conquest. We have become unaccustomed to such language today. And yet, had barbarians conquered civilized nations, as the Mongols conquered China or Persia, the brutality would have been no less. What interested Tocqueville, leaving aside the terminology of civility and barbarism, was the qualitative consequences of conquest. The usual mode, when "barbarians" overrun "civilization," is for the former to invite the latter into their newly stolen palaces and for the latter to open their schools to the new masters. Toynbee has made essentially the same observation, using a larger body of historical evidence and fancier language.

"But," Tocqueville observed, "when the side that has the physical force has intellectual superiority too, it is rare for the conquered to become civilized; they either withdraw or are destroyed." There are two ways of being destroyed: either physically or by changing from "barbarian" to "civilized." So far as Aboriginal people are concerned, when they become members of Canadian society, they also become citizens. And yet we know from our own experience that Aboriginal people claim to be more than another ethnic group. Why? Because they arrived in North America first? But the history of humanity is as much one of displacement of peoples as it is of permanence: why should the Dene or the Mohawks be exceptional when the Visigoths or the Qipchaq were pushed out? Because they never were conquered? Does anyone seriously maintain that Aboriginal peoples did not submit in one way or another to European sovereigns or to their successors? Let us be serious.

The answers to these rhetorical questions are obvious. The continuous existence of Aboriginal peoples as something more than ethnic stones in the multicultural mosaic is based not upon spurious historical and legal arguments, though these devices are often used today. It is based, rather, on Aboriginal experience and pride. We have begun with Tocqueville, so let us continue with him. His observations could certainly be augmented by the self-interpretation of Aboriginal people themselves, or by the remarks of sympathetic anthropologists or others, but it would be difficult to improve on his insights.

The central feature of Aboriginal experience, as of other pastoral nomads, was the hunt. With few exceptions, agriculture was despised. "No Indian in his bark hut is so wretched," Tocqueville said, "that he does not entertain a proud conception of his personal worth.... He thinks hunting and war the only cares worthy of a man." Tocqueville finds it amazing that such miserable individuals cherish "the same ideas and opinions as the medieval noble in his castle, and he only needs to become a conqueror to complete the resemblance." Aboriginals, then, are aristocrats. It is their wretched poverty that distinguishes them from European aristocrats, not their barbarism or savagery. Matthew Arnold made similar observations with respect to the British aristocracy of Victorian times, whom he also called barbarians.

Life in freedom in the forest may have been wretched, but Aboriginal hunters felt inferior to no one. But entering upon the sedentary civilization of Europeans, the Aboriginals entered poor and ignorant into, in Tocqueville's words, "a society where knowledge and wealth prevail. Having led an adventurous life, full of afflictions and dangers but also full of proud emotions, he must submit to a monotonous, obscure, and degraded existence." To illustrate the attractiveness of pride, nobility, and wretched aristocratic existence, Tocqueville summarizes the story of John Tanner:

> Tanner was a European who was carried off by the Indians at the age of six, and stayed for thirty years in the forests with them. Nothing can be more terrible than the afflictions he describes. He tells us of tribes without a chief, families without a nation, isolated men, the wrecks of powerful tribes, wandering at random through the ice and snow and desolate solitudes of Canada. Hunger and cold are their companions, and every day seems likely to be their last. Among such men mores have lost their sway, and traditions are powerless. Men become more and more barbarous. Tanner shares all these afflictions; he knows his European origin; it is not force that keeps him away from the white men; on the contrary, he goes every year to trade with them, enters their houses, and sees their comfort; he knows that any day that he wished to go back to civilized life he could easily do so, and he stays thirty years in the wilderness. When he does in the end return to civilized society, he confesses that the existence whose

afflictions he has described has secret charms which he cannot define;
he returned to it again and again after he had left it, and only with a
thousand regrets could tear himself away from so many afflictions.
And when he was finally settled among the white men, several of his
children refused to share his tranquillity and comfort.

One can transfer at least some of Tocqueville's insights into the
present day. No one who has had much experience of hunting can
doubt its barbarism. The opponents of hunting are forever point-
ing it out, *urbi et orbi*, so why should it not proudly be acknowledged? But our modern spokespersons for civilization forget the
other experiences that accompany the undoubted barbarism of the
hunt. Who, going armed into the woods or up a coulee, would
deny the immediacy of the experience of freedom? Hunters,
whether Aboriginal or, like Tanner, European, are indeed filled
with "proud emotions." An inevitable accompaniment of such
pride and freedom is gratitude when game is taken. Why? Because
as the contemporary Spanish philosopher Ortega y Gasset
observed in his *Meditations on Hunting*, there is never enough game.
Accordingly, when it arrives, it arrives as a gift. The appropriate
response to gracious acts is gratitude. This complex of experiences
is human, not Aboriginal. The conclusion we are compelled to
make is that Aboriginal spirituality, like Aboriginal pride, grows
from or is nourished by experiences that are common to non-Abo-
riginals as well.

The political implications of the demands for particular collective rights by Aboriginals, advanced on the grounds of their special
spirituality, are identical to those made by French Quebeckers on
the grounds of their special nationalism. As we mentioned earlier,
in this respect Trudeau was right: no one makes treaties with fellow citizens. If Aboriginals are serious about the "inherent right to

self-government," for example, Canadians can respond to this assertion of pride by recalling their own interests: if Aboriginals are citizens, why should their fellow citizens pay for the preservation of a culture not their own? If Aboriginals are not citizens, then the same question arises. The matter of Aboriginal citizenship is complex, because it contains two incompatible principles. Canadians are citizens because they are born in Canada (or are naturalized) and not because of their ethnicity. This is known in international law as the *jus soli*, the law of the soil. Aboriginals, or, to be more precise, Indians, are Indians on the basis of something like *jus sanguinis*, the law of blood. It is on this basis that Khanawake band councillor Billy Two Rivers recently spoke of the "genetic damage" done by intermarriage of his people with non-Indians.

Canada has an interest in such matters, even if it is little more than a financial one. On occasion, however, as when Canadian Armed Forces transport planes are shot at by Mohawks, then pride as well as interest is involved. As journalist Lysiane Gagnon observed with shame, "where else would a group of people involved in black-market activities and armed with illegal weapons be allowed to shoot at the army?" In this instance, clearly, Mohawk pride has been purchased with the shame of the Canadian army — or rather, the pusillanimity of Canadian politicians.

The absence of pride has caused our constitutional failures in the following way. Successive governments have tried to create a substitute for pride by focusing on the creation of a "national identity," on Canadianism, and on what we have called collectivist public virtue. But there is no substitute for pride. What they *have* created is an out-of-control public debt driven by an absurd welfare state. Where the citizens lack pride, governments are incapable of serving their true interests. That is why, though there are many poor but proud countries in the world, Canada is virtually alone in being rich and dependent.

ety." Sometimes, as we have seen, state action is necessary to protect and shelter civil society — most notably in war and times of turmoil. But not in times of peace. Then state action, state intervention in our lives, can only remove responsibility from citizens. Then its redistributive adventures can only reward failure and punish success.

The effect would be to get us out of our tax quagmire: current government spending leads to higher taxes, particularly taxes higher than are levied in the United States. Canadians take corrective measures such as tax avoidance that result in lower government revenues and a bureaucratically driven demand for higher taxes. And around we go again. Studies in the European Economic Community have shown that a 4 per cent differential in Value Added Tax between countries is an incentive to smuggling. Is it any wonder that smuggling is not only in Canadians' individual interest but has become a source of pride, and not just for Mohawks? With welfare policies cut, our deficits will be eliminated; with privatization, assets can be applied against the debt. Once those steps are taken, is there any reason why Canada should not become a tax haven? Why should we not attract industry north of the border because of our low taxes instead of sending it south because of our high taxes?

Internal markets for health care and schools would bring great discipline to bear upon two administrative organizations that are devoid of any incentive structures. In the health system, for example, there is nothing stopping over-demand by patients and over-servicing by physicians. The answer is clear: user fees. The difficulties with schools are so many that it is hard to know where to begin. Probably the most effective improvements can come, at least in the short term, by attacking — yes, attacking — teachers' unions. The main things that teachers seem to want are smaller classes and more money. Larger classes and less money would mean two things: first, only individuals who were dedicated to teaching would enter a classroom, and second, once inside they would have to discipline students, an imperative that would quickly bring an end to such proven stupidities as child-centred learning and feel-good education.

The question that haunts all politicians in liberal democracies is: are you better off? As the British experience of privatization indicates, the proposals we have just outlined will probably not command popular support in advance. Some readers may even be bold to discover that such proposals are "right-wing," whatever that is supposed to mean. The fact is, however, that *after* privatization in Britain, after the practical benefits have become evident to everyone, the Labour party has ceased to threaten to undo what privatization has wrought. And for good reason: it works. It serves the interests of citizens and taxpayers and so has earned their support.

In the short term, however, the appeal must be made to pride as well as to interest. Virtue, we know, is a fine thing, but we also know from Machiavelli, the great teacher of all modern politicians, that virtue is secured more by the dislike of one's enemies than the gratitude of one's friends. But surely we need not look very far to find vicious minorities to blame for having landed us in our mess.

The failures of Meech Lake and of the Charlottetown Accords, especially the latter, showed that Canadian citizens blamed their political leaders and the celebrated opinion leaders, both in the media and on other commanding heights. Indeed, the last election was nothing if not a vote against the politicians and their policies that have led us into the quagmire. Are not Canadians proud of having repudiated the Charlottetown Accord and the architect of Meech Lake?

We think it is entirely possible that Canadians are capable of taking pride in their country. Indeed, we have modest expectations that a form of "national" pride may emerge as an unintended and perhaps unobtrusive consequence of the way we handle our current social and economic problems, as well as the Quebec question and the Aboriginal question. A quiet pride in being Canadian is well known in our lore. On occasion, in foreign parts, for instance, pride in Canada is often a real experience, and an experience of Canadian reality. We contrast ourselves, as Canadians, with noisy Americans and even noisier Australians. Canadians abroad under arms have done so from the time of Lord Strathcona's Horse. One could imagine a quiet pride in our constitutional order as well. The first step, we believe, is to stop rewarding failure and penalizing success. After having taken that step, what is to stop us from noble actions?